READYALREADY

The Future-Ready Mindset to Keep Up,
Stand Out, and Shape What's Next

by

ALLISTER FROST

READYALREADY

The Future-Ready Mindset to Keep Up, Stand Out, and Shape What's Next

This publication is designed to provide accurate and authoritative information regarding the subject matter covered. It is sold with the understanding that the publisher is not engaged in rendering legal, accounting, or other professional services. If you require legal advice or other expert assistance, you should seek the services of a competent professional.

Design and cover art by Peaceful Profits.

ReadyAlready is the registered trademark of Wild Orange Media Ltd.

Paperback ISBN: 978-1-967587-08-7
Hardback ISBN: 979-8-262209-30-9
eBook ISBN: 978-1-967587-09-4

*'Life's a journey,
not a destination.'*

Aerosmith

For

Angela, and Finn and Eryn x

Contents

Preface

I bet you have been through a lot of changes in your lifetime. When you got your first job or started school, each new assignment may have seemed like an insurmountable challenge. If your early working days were anything like mine, you got lost on the way to the canteen and then again, even more embarrassingly, on the way back to your own desk. But you figured things out, you learned the ropes, and with every new experience, you grew more confident and capable. Maybe your professional past looked something like this: In a moment of personal triumph, you raised a smile when a colleague said, "You're really good at your job now!" The boss was happy with your work too, so they encouraged you to take on a bigger role with even more responsibility. They even asked you to show the latest batch of new recruits around the company, and colleagues started turning to you for advice. You took pride in your work and became the go-to person everyone wanted to see and be seen with. A promotion came your way; more money, better rewards. The future was looking bright. All those years of dedication and hard work were finally paying off.

But then you came to a fork in the road. Colleagues began talking about new ways of doing things. Some said they thought the company could save time and money by adopting new processes. The water cooler conversations shifted to a new system to track sales. You heard about a competitor who was already making waves with new sales channels and innovative customer service techniques. Back when I was at Microsoft (which I'll tell you much more about later), we faced unexpected obstacles almost every week. But when we shifted our mindset, the obstacles became opportunities.

Faced with the need to change, you were smart and realised it was time for some fresh thinking and ideas.

Perhaps you've experienced challenges in your career where, with hindsight, you now realise your company papered over the cracks when really what it needed was to fix the foundations. For example, perhaps you spotted an opportunity for your company to communicate better with its customers. You did some research, evaluated your options, and gathered advice from experts. It was tough wrapping your head around newfangled ways of working, and even harder getting your colleagues excited about the extra workload the changes would create. Even as the rollout of your fancy Customer Relationship Management (CRM) system began, you weren't sure if you were steering the ship towards open seas or the cliffs! Mercifully, things went well. Great job: you were back in the game.

And it worked, for a while. But things kept changing. As soon as your team mastered one new CRM technique, a better solution appeared. Every new initiative seemed more confusing and disruptive. Even the company's most junior recruits were now asking questions you couldn't answer! How you yearned for the good old times, when you would cruise through the working day on a reassuring bed of experience and certainty.

Now, some days at work feel like you're running on a hamster wheel that some invisible, evil force is spinning faster each day. There are more changes coming, more learning curves to climb, more seemingly impossible transformations to deliver. By the end of each day, you're exhausted, juggling projects and priorities. And no matter how many hours you work, it feels like your work is never done. You can't go on like this. Something needs to change and fast.

This is exactly why I'm writing this book. I never want you to feel behind again. Instead, I want you to be **ReadyAlready** for whatever life throws at you! I'll show you how to embrace a Future-Ready Mindset and start creating the bright future that you deserve.

Introduction

This book is a guide to help you thrive in a fast-changing workplace, turn novelty into advantage, and create the brilliant future you deserve at work and beyond.

Feeling that you have fallen behind the times can feel frustrating. Most of us like to think we've still got it. We know the best way to get stuff done, and we finish most days having made a valuable contribution. But it is becoming harder than ever to keep up with the workload, the constant changes, and to stay on top of your to-do list, feeling like you've made a positive difference.

The cause of change lies largely, but not exclusively, in scientific and technological progress. Every new invention—from the non-stick frying pan to the smartphone—ushers in new ways to live and work. One moment, you're calling your friend from the landline to let them know you got home safely, the next you're having a video chat with them all the way home in the back of a self-driving car.

Technology moves fast, but the changes it brings to our lives are not always as easy to detect or navigate—they can be slow and creeping. To properly appreciate how much change you are living through, it's often easier to compare yourself to previous generations. The differences in our lives with those of our parents and grandparents are clear to see.

Each new advance ushers in more change. Progress invites more progress, and the pace of change accelerates. And so, each day you are confronted by shifting working practices and new ways to live your life. Keeping up with everything is virtually impossible, so you have to make choices about what to pay attention to and what to ignore. But if you allow yourself to fall behind, you risk missing out on new opportunities and becoming less useful in both your workplace and your community.

But I bring good news! Obsolescence need not be your destiny. You *can* swim happily with the seas of change. This book will help you keep up and stay relevant at work and at home. It will arm you with a mindset of positivity, self-belief, and some fun, daily habits. My goal is simple: to empower you to enjoy a lifetime of growth and positive change. I call this having a Future-Ready Mindset. But more on that later…

From Small Beginnings

Think of this: Each time you are confronted by a new challenge, you have an opportunity to learn new things. Over time, you've grown into a proficient and independently competent person. But, however capable you have become, it's unlikely that every skill you have gained through life is still as useful as it once was. In some aspects, previous generations had it easier. With limited opportunities to move between different professional workplaces or industries, or to experience diverse global cultures, a 'job for life' was commonplace, and many people enjoyed relative lifetime stability. Our world today is very different. Human progress, along with scientific innovations that exponentially accelerate technology, means you are now likely to transition through dozens of jobs, homes, and experiences during your lifetime. In fact, only a tiny fraction of the knowledge you gained in your first year as an adult will still be relevant in your last. These days, lifelong learning is essential, and you're unlikely to excel with only the education from your college days or a training course you completed five years ago. Having a growth mindset and knowing that your abilities can constantly improve over time may help you to surf the waves of change. But a growth mindset alone is not enough.

Enter the Future-Ready Mindset

In this book, I will share a simple, powerful process to help you make continuous transformation your personal superpower for life. I will show you how to make friends of novelty and change, so you are always excited to stretch your comfort zone to embrace positive opportunities for growth. With a rekindled passion for adventure and learning, you'll feel energised to explore fresh possibilities and fulfil your true career potential. And I'll encourage you to share your newfound passion for change with others, so you win their support and can spread the joy of being future-ready for life.

Early in my working life, long before personal computers were a thing, I was sent on a two-day training course to learn how to give a presentation using an overhead projector (OHP). If you've never come across an OHP, it was all we had before the invention of the powerful little projectors we now use in conference rooms, home theatres, and gaming. An OHP was a hefty beige metal box housing a powerful lightbulb that could project an image onto a wall or screen. It looked like a primitive Soviet-era periscope, and in the 1990s you'd find one of these marvels of modern technology in nearly every conference or meeting room.

And, yes, you did read that correctly: It took me two full days of classes to learn how to use an OHP. In fairness, my fellow trainees and I did learn a wonderful technique for overlaying each transparency slide (if you know, you know!) before revealing the next, much like the 'wipe' transition in your favourite presentation software, but with more swagger and footwork. Mastery of the OHP required learning how to speak eloquently while switching transparency slides, ideally without inflicting irreparable eye damage on the audience by accidentally blinding them with the light.

By the end of day two, my transitions between overhead transparencies were almost balletic and, if challenged, I could probably still do a half-decent job of projecting information on a wall with little more than some clear plastic sheets and a dangerously hot lamp.

But the majesty of my technique was never going to be enough to keep this skill from becoming utterly redundant just a few years later. Instead, an easier, newer method became available. Today, you are more likely to connect your laptop to a tiny portable projector or to cast slides to a wall-mounted TV from your tablet, or even to share your screen directly to someone's smartphone over wi-fi. Anyone who still insists on using an OHP today is living in the past. And while it's probably also true that their stubborn dedication to outdated presentation techniques might just prove more entertaining than many of the dire PowerPoint presentations we sit through, there's really no place for an OHP today!

The OHP is a defunct tool that reminds us how rapidly our world can change. But it's not just tools and technology that can fall out of favour; the skills we hold can also become redundant. Right now, if you think about a typical day and how you complete routine tasks, you could probably find more efficient ways to get almost everything done. You just haven't had time—or maybe the inclination—to develop new skills or make the leap yet.

Here's how you can think about life and learning differently. We all grew up imagining that the skills we acquire are ours for the keeping. The education system instils this mindset into us early on by encouraging us to memorise information for later recall in an examination. Academic success is, to a large extent, a measure of how well we understand information and how precisely we can recall it. Logically, the retention of information would seem the most useful outcome of education but, as we all quickly realise as adults, there's precious little value in knowing who signed the Magna Carta or the precise wording of Pythagoras' Theorem. Practical knowledge that can help us in the real world is far more useful.

Your Leaky Bucket and the Future-Ready Mindset

Memorising facts or developing specialist skills rarely delivers as much value to us in the long term as it does in the here and now. And that's why I invite you to imagine any skills or special abilities you hold not as lifelong possessions, but as items swirling around your brain in a leaky old bucket. Yes, a skillset bucket, in your brain, that leaks. The sort of leaky bucket that you might look at and think, 'Oh no, that's no use to anyone, throw it away!' The sort of bucket you might even hesitate to grab in an emergency if your best friend was on fire. And, inside that leaky bucket, you'll find all the wonderful lessons you have learned on your journey through life. Useful stuff like how to reboot your computer, how to schedule a meeting, or how to secretly apply for a new job without your boss finding out. Lots of useful information—the net result of a lifetime of learning. In addition, out of the bottom of the bucket, you can see your outdated knowledge and expertise slowly seeping away with the passage of each day.

But why do some skills leak away? It's simple: many of your hard-learned skills will be of no value in the future.

Just like my astonishing flamboyance with an OHP, some of your skills may now be past their use-by date. The leaky bucket of your mind silently and relentlessly lets go of the outdated skills to make room for ones that provide value for the future. And, in so doing, it frees up space for more useful, up-to-date, or even future-ready skills.

Some people choose to fight back against the leaky bucket by stubbornly relying only on well-established ways of working and refusing to explore alternatives. This may not be a bad choice to make; after all, some of the old ways are still the best. But, in most instances, doggedly relying on approaches that are past their best is unlikely to make you first choice when a new project or opportunity comes along at work. And while your resistance to change may temporarily slow the leakage, it's unlikely that you'll ever be able to revive a fading, redundant skill into a sustainable solution that will serve you in the future. It's inevitable and there's no escape; no matter how brilliantly you can convert a faxed sales report into a colourful pie chart, the universe will ultimately decide if this skill should stay or leak away. The bucket is a-leakin' and the times they are a-changin'.

But take comfort; we're all in this together! Your bucket is just as leaky as mine and those of everyone around you. No one is immune. Just being aware of the leak gives you an opportunity to start exploring alternatives. So, instead of lamenting the demise of old skills, like knowing how to make a call with a rotary phone or how to read a printed bus timetable, perhaps you could view their passing as a joyful opportunity for personal reinvention and a chance to discover how to make life better than you ever previously thought possible.

Fighting this leaky bucket by hoping you can plug the holes is largely futile so, instead, I recommend you celebrate it every day! Simply knowing that it is OK to leave old, outdated skills behind can free up your mind to explore what's new. It's also a great way to gain a lead over competitors—and even work colleagues—by accelerating the demise of the past and latching on to the new.

But if the bucket is leaky, isn't there a risk that some valuable, hard-earned skills might slip through, too? Thankfully, that's not the case. The most up-to-date, future-relevant skills are too substantial to fall through the cracks. While they remain of value, they will be safe in the bucket. Only skills whose time has passed can leak out, usually without warning, and always without ceremony.

Some people fall into the trap of thinking their current value is only the sum of their past experiences. But this is short-sighted and ignores the most valuable skill of all: the ability to adapt and adjust to what the future may require. That's why coming to terms with this leaky bucket concept can be both joyful and liberating. It's a great feeling knowing that you're already prepared for tomorrow, when skills like knowing how to get cash from an ATM, fill a car with petrol, or hand-write and post a birthday card will soon be as archaic as using an OHP.

So, abandon any false notions you may once have held that the past was a golden era that we should perpetuate and replicate. The past was what it was, but now you have something new to explore. And humbly accept that you don't have all the answers or know for sure what the future may bring. With this enlightened perspective, you can begin a new journey of learning and discovery and begin exploring the limitless horizon of fresh possibilities that a Future-Ready Mindset can bring.

Who needs a Future-Ready Mindset anyway?

A leaky bucket leaks, that much we know. Faced with this unstoppable, lifelong loss of outdated skills, the only way to remain useful in the workforce, and your community, is to top up your bucket regularly with new skills. That means committing to personal development so you will be ready for the very different future that lies ahead. It's no longer enough to excel only in the present; you also need to look out for emerging possibilities and be ready to grab them in pursuit of your goals.

The result of committing to purposeful, future-facing, lifelong learning is having a Future-Ready Mindset. It's a skill that is rarely taught in business schools or company training programmes, but is now a must-have for long-term success.

A Future-Ready Mindset emerges from a continuous cycle of discovery, learning, and forward thinking to identify, de-risk, and ultimately introduce changes that will benefit your future.

> Or, to put it even more simply: **A Future-Ready Mindset is a proactive approach to thinking and planning that prepares you for the inevitable changes and challenges of the future.**

When mindsets go wrong

If you work for a large company, you may have colleagues who work in a Research and Development (R&D) department, or maybe an Innovation Team. These forward-thinking groups may be tasked with bringing new ideas into the organisation, evaluating their merits, and developing them into new products or services. With all this future-ready thinking going on, who could blame you for feeling that it is not your responsibility to bring new ideas to the business? You've already got a long to-do list anyway; someone else can worry about the future!

Or maybe you work in a medium-sized company, where you are used to taking direction from your manager or perhaps the company owner. From your relatively junior position you can relax knowing that their brilliant business minds will be constantly scanning the horizon for smart ways to improve results. You'll find out what needs to change when the time is right, or when someone gets round to telling you.

Or perhaps you run your own small business. You're already busier than a bee on a windy day and don't have time to think far beyond the present. Business survival is the name of the game, and you have learned to roll with each crisis as it rears its ugly head. You've too much on your plate; there aren't enough hours in the day to introduce more innovative ways of working. The closest you have to a plan is hoping that your future will happen—frankly just that would be a win!

Whatever your situation, none of these mindsets will serve you well in the long term. All the evidence of my work with hundreds of companies and business leaders points to one vital truth: If you want to stay relevant and useful in the workforce, you have to take responsibility for your own future. And no one gets a pass on this; we're all individually responsible for creating our own pathway through life. Besides, who could be better at shaping your future than you?

Many of the changes you will face in your lifetime are inevitable. They will happen whether you like them or not. Just as your smartphone has superseded your Filofax, an artificial intelligence robot may one day replace your smiling company receptionist. Learning to anticipate the likely inevitability of some changes is important because it buys you time to think ahead and plan for an unavoidable disruption before it turns your life upside down. You won't always correctly identify every inevitability, but you'll be right much of the time. Many of the challenges you will encounter will be relatively easy to predict though. Just as trends like remote work, automation, and the gig economy are reshaping today's workplace, longer-term shifts—like robotics, a cashless society, and the move to sustainable energy—could bring equally big changes. Learning to anticipate the inevitable may help you to stay relevant and valuable in the workforce for many years to come.

Thankfully, you don't have to be one of those mystic fortune tellers with a ceremonial crystal ball to develop a Future-Ready Mindset. All you need is a little thinking space and some time for exploration and ideation. This book will guide you through the process step by step and help you discover fresh possibilities for your amazing future. And, as you'll soon discover, you really can be ready for whatever life may throw at you.

Who is this book for?

This book is for everyone who wants to realise their full potential in the face of the relentless changes tomorrow will bring. It will be helpful to you at work and play; use it to shape your life as you wish. The techniques you will learn will help you develop your career, lead a team towards new success, and make you the go-to person who's not only adaptable to change, but whose mind is at the forefront of emerging possibilities and future trends.

The World Economic Forum predicts that two-thirds of today's schoolchildren will grow up to do jobs that don't yet exist. And around half of the activities that people are paid to perform today will soon be automated thanks to advances in artificial intelligence and clever robotics. With so many workers facing dramatic changes to their jobs—or even complete job obsolescence—there is huge demand for people with a personal hunger for growth coupled with the future-facing skills we will need in the new world of work. This 'Fourth Industrial Revolution', where the physical and digital worlds collide, will have a profound impact on all of humanity. There is simply no better time to seize the positive opportunities that continuous, unstoppable change will bring to your life.

My hope is that this little book will give you the hunger and motivation to ensure your skillset bucket never runs dry. You may have already dreamed about that joyful moment—perhaps surrounded by sobbing colleagues at your extremely well-attended retirement party—when you can finally say, 'I'm no longer going to bother keeping up!' Let's park that dream right here, because no matter how radically your world may change, you *can* continue to make a useful contribution in the workplace and to your community for as long as you choose. You don't have to give up, even after retirement. Developing a Future-Ready Mindset may mean you waste less time lazing in your comfort zone and enjoy many more years to pursue and realise new opportunities for personal growth and success.

What qualifies me to write this book?

This book is the synthesis of my work as a business transformation expert and marketing specialist. It brings together much of what I have learned about change and keeping up in this fast-evolving world.

Over the three decades of my career, I have launched new products and global advertising campaigns for Kimberly-Clark and Microsoft. I've also helped spark new thinking at brilliant companies like GE HealthCare, 3M, and Vodafone. Experience has taught me the importance of how we think about change and ways to leverage it as a tool for long-term success. For my keynote talks and training masterclasses, I have codified a process that began to form in my mind while helping my colleagues stay ahead of the curve at Microsoft. The result is a simple, five-step process that will shape and inspire your Future-Ready Mindset.

How to read this book

This book contains everything you need to broaden your horizon so that you can become future-ready for life. With each page you read, you will develop and enhance your Future-Ready Mindset using a simple five-step process called the **ReadyAlready Growth Cycle.**

It's a powerful, repeatable process that will quickly become a routine part of your everyday life. Think of it as a good personal habit that you haven't yet formed. At the heart of the cycle is your **Personal Mission** (PM). This is the heartfelt reason why you do what you do, usually in the service of others. Pinning down your PM can be tricky, so you'll have an entire chapter to explore this topic and think about the impact you have on

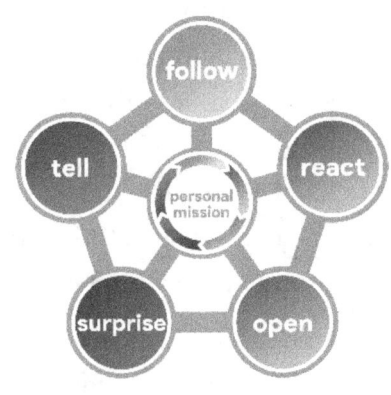

others and the remarkable value that you bring to the world. Everything that follows in the cycle should align with both your PM and the goals of any jobs you may hold. That's why it is so important that you identify your Personal Mission first.

The five-step cycle then introduces you to each of the five steps in turn: **FOLLOW, REACT, OPEN, SURPRISE,** and **TELL.** The order of the steps is important and easy to remember. The initial letters spell my surname, FROST. You can read about each of these steps in their respective chapters and decide how they can help you get ahead and deliver your Personal Mission. I have also provided exercises for key steps in the cycle, so you can start thinking and applying what you discover right away. Your future really starts now!

If you're anything like me, you may feel tempted to skip the exercises. After all, you're not at school anymore! But please do give them some thought. The answers you uncover and the conclusions you reach will be unique and valuable to you, and within them may lie the keys to a bright future of new possibilities. There's no time limit to this process either and you should take as long as you feel you need. In fact, I'd encourage you to take a few days out between chapters to give yourself time to explore each exercise and ponder more deeply what each step means for you.

By the end of this book, you will have found a powerful, repeatable technique for discovering, exploring, and exploiting new possibilities for your future. This will be an intensely personal quest as you lay the foundations for the future you deserve. You can complete most of the cycle on your own, although, as you'll see in the final step, TELL, it's a whole lot easier to gather support for change when you share your discoveries with others. I'll provide examples from my life along the way, and you will decide how to maximise the benefits for you.

The future is yours to create. You, and only you, are best placed to decide how to make it a reality. Are you ready to get started? Of course you are! In fact, you're better than ready; you're **ReadyAlready,** as you'll discover in the next chapter.

See you in the next few pages,

Allister x

Part 1

EMPOWER YOURSELF FOR FUTURE SUCCESS

CHAPTER 1

THE CASE FOR A FUTURE-READY MINDSET

With constant change and uncertainty defining our world, complacency in your 9 to 5 or your approach to work will be your undoing. In fact, all the evidence of my work with hundreds of companies and business leaders points to one vital truth: If you want to stay relevant and useful in the workforce (and employed), you've got to take responsibility for your own future. No one gets a pass on this; we're all individually responsible for creating our own path, both professionally and personally. If you're not coming up with new ideas or seeing yourself as an active change agent within your company, you're not keeping your job safe. In fact, you may be inadvertently announcing to the world that you're already past your best-before date!

Besides, who could be better at shaping your future than you?

Welcome to the Future-Ready Mindset, a step-by-step process that will help you discover fresh possibilities for your amazing future. Think of it as preparing the rest of your life for long-term success and happiness. With the Future-Ready Mindset, you will be personally focused on meeting change head-on instead of trying to ignore or deflect it. You'll find there's more joy and confidence in carving your own path, all while using a method that will keep you motivated and productive.

I first came up with the expression 'Future-Ready Mindset' after years of finding myself crashing onto the shores of continuous change. While there was no single moment where this all fell into place, I recognised the need for this solution when I was working in the Central Marketing Group of Microsoft. Each day, I was grasping to make sense of what was going on, whilst racing between back-to-back meetings. My early career with a global manufacturing company hadn't prepared me well for the dizzying pace of change in the technology sector. It was intense! Company leaders spewed new ideas at a chaotic pace, often for no seemingly rational reason. We were doing Plan A, then U-turning to Plan B, and sometimes even back again before the day was out.

When I began implementing the Future-Ready Mindset, my team and I focused on trying to do one thing brilliantly rather than five things to a mediocre standard. We learned not to get caught up in the excitement and hype of the new, but instead paused to analyse what we were doing. We were humble about our skills, but intensely curious about what might come of them. We dreamed big and became very good at sharing our ideas generously, and then we collaborated closely to make our ideas the best they could be.

Thanks to three decades of learning and experience, I've managed to decode how this system can work for professionals in almost any industry. In fact, I've launched new products and global advertising campaigns for Kimberly-Clark and, of course, Microsoft. I've also helped spark new thinking at brilliant companies like Philips, Cisco, Bosch, and Airbus. Experience has taught me the importance of *how* we think about change and how we can exploit change as fuel for our long-term success. For my keynote talks and training masterclasses, I have perfected the mindset process I first developed to help me keep up with the curve at Microsoft. The result is a simple, five-step process that will inform and inspire your Future-Ready Mindset.

As a result of the Future-Ready Mindset, which I've experienced firsthand and seen with my own clients, you will see these measurable benefits:

- **Improved mental health.** As I discovered, your emotional well-being will be strengthened when you feel less anxious about change, uncertainty, or things not going your way. You can take more bumps in your stride and cope better with whatever comes at you.

- **More energy to work collaboratively and creatively.** Positivity and confidence are contagious (in a good way). People will want to collaborate with you—and you with them—because we're all attracted to people who walk confidently towards opportunity rather than shy away from it.

- **Business growth.** In addition to emotional and relational benefits, a Future-Ready Mindset can help you get your message to more and more people. While, of course, this will vary, your confidence to greet change head-on may one day show in your bank balance. To be clear, you shouldn't follow this process to get rich. You need to embark on this solution because you want to live a full, happy life, doing useful stuff in the service of others. In the process, though, you will naturally benefit yourself. As an example, I'm continuously improving what I do, allowing me to keep my offer at the top of the market. I've always got something exciting bubbling away for my future that may one day be of value to myself and others. Do the work first, and fame and fortune may follow.

In addition to my success supporting hundreds of companies, I've heard from countless busy professionals like you. After my talks and coaching workshops, I'm excited to see how much some audience members begin to think differently, share their fresh ideas, and express a renewed energy to do their best work. People tell me how the Future-Ready Mindset has awakened their own personal and professional desire to improve, perhaps regaining that exciting 'buzz' they felt at the start of their careers, before their spark was beaten out of them through exhausting years climbing the career ladder.

One of my favourite stories came from a senior manager who was six months away from retirement. He came up to me and said that because of what I spoke on about the Future-Ready Mindset, he now felt inspired to make the most out of his last six months of employment. In fact, to use his words, he was determined to 'Make everyone at work feel really sad when I eventually go, rather than glad to see the back of me!' This man realised he could contribute so much more to his company before he entered his 'golden years'. Of course, you don't have to be of retirement age to start feeling this way; go to work today and give it your all! Then, a domino effect may happen, where your desire to find new opportunities becomes infectious to others. And, enthused by your example, your co-workers may even continue to build a positive, supportive work culture long after you've clocked out for the last time. Someone has to be the first domino—why not you?

The core principle behind the Future-Ready Mindset is this: it's all about you. A company only grows when the individuals within it grow—and it starts with you. Everything in this process should be driven by your personal desire to be as productive and inventive as you can be. Truly, your best future cannot be created from the top down. Leaders, no matter how brilliant, won't instil self-motivation in you, that's your job. Instead, you'll need to believe you're the best person to create your future so you effectively become your own boss. In turn, the place you work and the people you work with will benefit more when you bring your unique perspective to the table. The company gets to tap into a diversity of ideas they, let's be honest, otherwise might have missed. They need you: they really do.

Look, let's be honest—and I hope I'm not being too forward here—your boss is as clueless about predicting or shaping the future as everyone else. And if you sit back waiting for someone else to take the initiative, you may soon struggle to comprehend what's going on, and you won't be keeping pace with innovation. You shouldn't wait for someone to tell you what to do next at the risk of their next words being, 'You're fired'. Instead, find the courage to make change happen, to create change, to be the change. I think you'll enjoy that feeling, and this book will show you how.

Try this: Rather than thinking, 'My company employs me to do a job', start thinking, 'I employ my company so I can do cool stuff I enjoy in the service of others'. Of course, we all need a job to pay the bills, but that is a lousy motivation if you want to do your best work and make a positive difference to the world. Think of it this way: Your employment gives you access to an environment where you can flourish. This is an enlivening way of thinking about your work. You cease to see yourself as a cog in a machine, but instead as a self-motivated entrepreneur who can achieve and do amazing things. You might not get a chance to, say, launch a new operating system, like I did with Microsoft, but you do have a privileged place where you can make your unique mark on the world.

An organisation thrives when each staff member is personally motivated, wants to be there, and knows they are making a difference, not just going through the motions. No one wins when they are reluctantly clocking in and excitedly clocking out. Feeling enthusiastic and optimistic about your ability to improve things will keep you motivated and help make the world a little better each day.

In the last year, through my guidance, many companies have discovered and begun implementing the Future-Ready Mindset. Here are some of the things I've been involved with:

- Helped a government agency department to successfully navigate an otherwise tumultuous restructuring. I gave them a positive outlook and the fresh mindset needed to cope with that change. And although most of their leadership team changed, the team was able to continue their important work and lay fresh foundations for a more efficient service in the future.

- Given college lecturers and support staff the energy to rethink their approach to education, so they can be in tune with students' changing needs. As a result, they are focused on keeping their teaching materials relevant, creating a better learning environment for young people, and, frankly, finding the energy to keep going through another turbulent academic year.

- Inspired a confectionery company to make the bold business model changes needed to double their market share.

- Helped a pharmaceutical company create new communication channels for patients going through cancer treatment, so they can offer more tailored support to both patients and their families. These teams do incredible, life-saving work.

- Worked with a big banking group to shorten response times with customers and inspire them to innovate faster and keep them on pace with the new financial tech players in their sector.

- Assisted a large construction company's staff. I helped the company's structural engineers and architects approach complex infrastructure projects with more curiosity about what's changing in other countries around the world, so they can design and build more future-facing developments for their clients.

As you're beginning to see, the Future-Ready Mindset is more than a process. It's actually a recipe for rediscovering your love of the new and creating the future you deserve. For me, I no longer get frustrated by things that are beyond my control. Now, I look at situations and say, 'Let's make the most of this; let's see the positives in this.' I make more time to reflect on what I can do better, not what others are doing badly. This solution takes a simple discipline of going through each day wondering what can I do and where should

I focus, so I'm constantly open to seeing where things can be made better. I'm also less scattergun with things. Instead, I do what matters most to me: my own agenda. Instead of getting pulled in multiple directions, I focus on making a positive difference that matters to me.

In this book, you'll discover a simple, structured approach with you at the very centre. It's all about you, which itself makes it super easy to learn and remember. There will be simple exercises you can do at your own pace. Think of it this way: I'll set the stages—you set the rhythm. I'd love for you to keep this book by your desk and go to it as a guide whenever you're stuck. If I'd had this book back at Microsoft, I might have achieved more and faster. I'm hoping to do this for you.

With a Future-Ready Mindset, you'll no longer get set in your ways or wait for others to be the innovators. You won't waste emotional energy feeling frustrated or even envious. You'll be less bothered by what other people say or do, and instead focus on your own thing. You'll also find yourself moaning less to your family (or anyone else who will listen!) about another tough day at work. You'll be more focused on what you *can* change, instead of what you can't control. You'll get to experiment and learn something new every day. Rather than experiencing change as a victim, you'll see it as an opportunity. You'll also try lots of little experiments that carry minimal risk, and less big change that feels hard. I hope you'll bounce out of bed each day, even on a Monday morning, keen to get on with meaningful work. And, you'll experience a profound personal renaissance of embracing and pursuing new possibilities in your day-to-day life.

This mindset will likely become part of what makes you *you*, as it has for me. In fact, I no longer have to remind myself to look for worthwhile improvements because this way of thinking has permeated so deeply into my mindset, sparking an almost instinctive reaction to any challenging situation. I hope to remain this way for as long as I choose to be active in the workforce, and to continue making a meaningful contribution to the world. I want this for you too.

Conclusion

The future is yours to create. You, and only you, are best placed to decide how to make it a reality. You have knowledge, skills, and ambition. It's time to share that with the world.

Are you ready—and perhaps excited—to get started? Of course you are! You're better than ready; you're ReadyAlready!

Along the way, be prepared for novelty and exploration. Get ready to feel excited by the future and the new possibilities you may soon discover.

Off we go!

Curious about how other people have benefited from using the ReadyAlready Growth Cycle at work? Check out these case studies and see how they did!

READYALREADY CASE STUDIES

Lisa worked at the head office of a large retail bank. She led a team of talented software developers who were tasked with introducing new features to the bank's mobile apps to improve customer experience. In recent years, multiple new competitors had entered the market with innovative digital-only banking solutions. These new players were proving popular and customer data showed that Lisa's once loyal customers were at risk of leaving the bank, enticed by attractive introductory offers and clever app features. Needing some fresh thinking in the team to speed up her bank's innovation pipeline, Lisa asked me to introduce her colleagues to the ReadyAlready Growth Cycle.

Several key team members were initially hesitant to consider new approaches to banking, preferring to stick to their existing approaches and skill sets. And many others were concerned that the bank's legacy technology infrastructure would prevent them from making meaningful improvements to their apps. However, by adopting an open-minded approach to the problem, the team quickly realised there were many suboptimal aspects to their current approach, some of which they could fix relatively quickly.

In a creativity session, one colleague dreamt up a way of making the existing app more streamlined by prioritising features that are used most often—a benefit that even the new banks didn't yet offer. And, in talking through the many new possibilities they had uncovered, the team found renewed excitement for improving the app, not simply protecting the status quo. As a result, Lisa's team halved the time from coming up with new ideas to beta testing them. That's a huge productivity gain. New features are now added to the app nearly every month, not roughly annually as happened before. And the bank's customers have countless good reasons to stay loyal and benefit from a more innovative, future-facing approach to digital banking.

Simon is a training manager for a large town council in the UK, with responsibility for supporting the development needs of several thousand frontline staff and managers. Faced with shrinking budgets and ever-rising workloads, he was no longer able to provide the training and development his colleagues needed to learn new skills. Several key team members had recently resigned and staff morale was taking a dive. I introduced the council to the ReadyAlready Growth Cycle to help Simon inspire his colleagues to think differently and identify leaner, less budget-draining ways they could keep up and learn.

As they reconsidered the council's approach to learning and development, several inefficiencies soon came to light as well as some intriguing new possibilities. One of Simon's colleagues learned how another regional council had developed an online programme to provide support and medical advice to pregnant women living in remote locations. He adapted that approach to provide virtual training for the council's home-based social workers.

Another colleague was so inspired, she decided to gift her team members a notebook and pen—paid for out of her own pocket!—and asked them to note down anything in their work that could potentially be done better or more efficiently. A few weeks later, her team met up to share over 20 brave new ideas for improvement, many of which they could implement immediately without incurring substantial costs.

By becoming more future-focused and innovative, the council now has a fresh approach to solving old problems with more creativity and clarity of purpose. And, most importantly, the town's residents are benefitting from better support from the council workers they depend upon. That's a very healthy return on investment for some fresh thinking and a few notebooks and pens!

Rob had been a Health & Safety (H&S) officer in the construction industry for over twenty years. Many of his colleagues see H&S as overburdensome and time-consuming, preferring wherever possible to 'just get on with the job', and not be slowed down by having to wear heavy protective clothing or carry out safety assessments before climbing ladders.

Rob empathised with his colleagues but knew that safety must always come first. However, getting his site-based colleagues to share this view always proved a challenge. Rob approached me to explore ways to make H&S more interesting at his company. Working through the ReadyAlready Growth Cycle, he realised that most employees were primarily motivated by completing their tasks in the shortest amount of time, not always by delivering the highest quality work—and sometimes at the expense of safety. Rob trained his teams on the benefits of having an interesting and compelling Personal Mission, helping them reconnect with the value their housing developments and shared spaces bring to local communities.

He then encouraged each construction worker to use their Personal Mission as inspiration to improve quality and make construction sites safer. Several team members offered invaluable insights into their work and helped Rob source better H&S equipment for their needs, while also reducing paperwork and admin. By questioning their current working practices, team members identified over a dozen easy workplace improvements that both saved time on site and reduced waste. The site teams now have a new shared sense of purpose and, most importantly, a safety record they are collectively proud of. They continue to meet regularly to share ideas and spot new opportunities for improvements, and H&S is no longer seen as a routine formality, but as a vital part of their work delivering a high quality end product to their customers.

CHAPTER 2

'I'M A PC' AND OTHER RADICAL IDEAS

My time at Microsoft informed my Future-Ready Mindset. Change was happening all the time and all around me in the company. Tech was being invented and reinvented on an almost daily basis. Our competitors were moving fast too, a constant reminder that we had to stay ahead of the game or risk falling behind. Within my role as a marketing professional, I had to be constantly aware of new ways to inform and inspire customers through mass communication channels like TV, press and social media.

Despite my experience and the level of sophistication in Microsoft's marketing teams, I was often confused about the right next steps for us as a company. This often led to feelings of randomness and uncertainty. It drove me to think:

We have to try new things, but where do we start?

Which of the dozens of pathways should we follow?

Should we keep doing what we know has worked before, or change course altogether?

This constant confusion sometimes resulted in not making decisions, or worse, making decisions all too hastily. Confused leaders and employees rarely make wise choices. And more often than not, in the fog of the unknown they tend to stick with what they already know, even if it's no longer working as well as hoped.

This was a deadly place for long-term business survival. Following Bill Gates' lead, I began to appreciate that change was coming at us faster and faster. The pace of innovation was likely to accelerate with each year, each quarter, each month. That's when I came to terms with what I truly need to do: stop lurching from one seemingly good idea to the next and instead try to get ahead of the game. As a company, we had to open ourselves to new possibilities to cope better with the dizzying array of challenges hurtling our way.

The most harrowing example of this was when we launched Windows Vista in January 2007. It was, by all accounts, an unmitigated disaster! Windows Vista was far too much change delivered far too quickly. It was the result, largely, of Microsoft resting on its laurels and not innovating in the preceding years. It was a belated overcorrection to finally put in the structural changes needed to create an operating system that could take full advantage of the power of the latest computer hardware. Despite sitting on a very healthy market share, Microsoft was failing to compete with Apple, and was losing the hearts and minds of people who had been loyal customers for years. And Apple, my arch-rival at the time, had been running those Mac versus PC ads, which you may remember.

The 'Get a Mac' ads laid out the shortcomings of Windows Vista in the form of a guy in a drab, grey suit (led in the USA by actor John Hodgman, and in the UK by David Mitchell), looking bland and rather dull. He had a PC. There was also an unflappably cool guy in the ad (played by actor Justin Long in the USA, and Robert Webb in the UK), who had an Apple Mac. He was hip without forcing it, just calm and in complete control of his life. It was a classic Steve Jobs' binary mindset: you can either be a Mac user or an idiot; you choose! That resonated loudly with a lot of people because Windows Vista was making their lives a misery, and many were hungry for better.

At this point, my team at Microsoft had to radically rethink what we were doing. We weren't going to win the hearts and minds of current and potential customers by continuing to do the same things. We decided to ditch conventional thinking and be bold and innovative. A major new campaign began quite deliberately with something really strange—a TV ad starring Bill Gates and comedian Jerry Seinfeld. It was zany and fun, and completely unexpected.

Watching Jerry help Bill trying on shoes in a discount store, and then requesting a computer that was 'delicious', was a deliberate distraction to make people sit up and pay attention. If we had simply carried on pushing ads that merely touted the latest version of Windows, people would have turned away. They'd been burnt before, weren't interested, and didn't have time for more empty promises. That's why we did something very different with Bill and Jerry: We ran three ads, all first appearing a few days apart to make everyone stop and pay attention. All this because we knew we had something much, much better in the wings.

Now that we had the world's attention, it was now time to unleash 'I'M A PC', a campaign featuring a plethora of real people and celebrities explaining how they use a PC in their daily lives. These were inventors, models, actors, adventurers, and teachers. Some were recognisable celebrities, but most were regular people living regular lives. It was a radical campaign that showed how real people from all walks of life relied on Windows to do important and sometimes extraordinary things. No fuss, no ceremony, just people using PCs to amazing effect. Windows users could get involved with the campaign too by creating and sharing their own 'I'M A PC' photos, videos, and conversations. This further underscored the fact that PCs were used all over the world, and that there was no 'shame' in being a PC user. In fact, using a PC was still pretty much universal, despite the impression Apple was eager to create. In an Internet first, we gave everyone access to an infinite video wall where they could upload their own photos and videos while saying, 'I'M A PC and I...' Some of these user-generated contributions even appeared in TV ads and billboards around the globe, and if you shared your video with a friend, they would start seeing you popping up in online ads! The campaign gave people a fresh and inspiring reason to rethink the role that computers and Windows could play in their lives. And, importantly for Microsoft, it put the 'Get a Mac' ads in the shade. Apple stopped running them a few weeks later. Job done!

By then, we had architected a much better product. The fault-ridden Windows Vista was now fit-for-purpose, and we were getting ready to roll out Windows 7. This is when we really got our mojo back: our self-belief. We were back on the front foot! Windows 7 paved the way for everything that has followed. Its ad campaign was confident and bold, giving computer users great reasons to give the latest version of Windows a try. Today, seventy per cent of computer users have a Windows PC compared to around twenty per cent using Apple. We showed the world how much they could achieve with Microsoft and created something radical and memorable. (Oh, and according to CNN, 'Get a Mac' actor Justin Long became a 'PC guy' in 2021.)

This new thinking worked for me and Microsoft, and the way we did this can help you too.

'How?' you may ask. Your approach to life needs to be more like the latest version of Windows than Windows Vista: expose yourself to gradual, continuous, minor improvements rather than risky, disruptive radical reinvention. Change doesn't need to be dramatic to be effective. Small, regular updates are the wise way to upgrade yourself. There's no advantage in holding back, then rushing to catch up by reinventing everything in one go. Windows Vista tried that, and it didn't end well!

Before fully embracing a Future-Ready Mindset, you may find yourself struggling to meet deadlines, hit targets, and even simply to keep up with the workload because you're being pulled in so many directions. You may have become reactive, or at the very least thrown into a passive state of, 'Everything's a struggle. It's too much. I give up.' Rather than being proactive about making choices or identifying new opportunities, you may be sitting there waiting anxiously for your boss's next madcap idea. Where's the fun in sitting back waiting for direction or letting others decide your destination? Surrendering control is incredibly stressful, anxiety-inducing, and risky. And it will probably prove futile in the end because you already know your boss's next idea probably won't work anyway! You need to find a way out of this perpetually reactive cycle.

Your turning point may look a bit like mine: You may realise it's really up to you to make good choices for the future. You need to be the one to identify what's right. Don't sit back and wait for someone senior to you to open their mouth and let the crazy spill out everywhere. Fully own that the only person who can best control your future or steer your future in the right direction is you! Anybody else will just be a poor substitute. You can have influence far beyond the parameters of your job title too. If you're thinking and looking, you can influence and inspire many people beyond your immediate work colleagues. How wonderful would it be to shape more of what matters? How freeing would it be to confidently voice a valid opinion and seize whatever opportunities arise? You can be the person in the room who creates the change. Make yourself indispensable, successful, and happy.

Where can this eventually land you? As a result of my mindset shift, I now have a far greater sense of control over the present—as you will too. You'll find a degree of serenity in your everyday work life that will elicit a sense of calm and spark eternal curiosity within you. You'll enjoy the benefits of the choices you've made and take full advantage of each moment. Like me, you may also discover a vivid excitement for the future, because you'll be always wondering, 'What's next?' You'll no longer be curious or excited in a randomised way. In fact, I'd venture to say you'll never run out of ideas, as you'll have an eternal hunger to explore new possibilities. You'll be excited in the present and motivated by the future. Instead of the 9 to 5 grind, you'll have a hopeful, curious, let's-do-it attitude.

These are the four specific improvements I have made to my business as a result of the Future-Ready Mindset, and you can too:

- **Consistently testing new sales and marketing techniques.** My customers' expectations are constantly changing, and there's so much learning that comes from that. We're always trying innovative things to connect with and help new people. This keeps our ideas fresh and up to date for the modern world.

- **Pushing new technology in intelligent ways.** We embrace new possibilities that come with technology, testing them carefully before placing our bets on what we believe may be the optimal solution for our needs.
- **Passionately sharing learnings.** I am very generous with my knowledge, helping others whenever I can. There are no secrets anymore, so making it difficult for people to get the help they need only means they will turn to someone else, not you. Personally, I take great pleasure now from sharing my knowledge to inspire people to be their best. This helps people find me as a thought leader, but also ensures that I too am learning every day. Imagine developing this level of confidence, and boldly putting your ideas on social media, podcasts, and the company intranet. These outlets can help you personally and professionally, while also supporting other people in their careers.
- **Pioneering new presentation and performance techniques.** Sometimes it's good to take your Future-Ready Mindset into a whole new arena. I've dabbled in stand-up comedy and improvisational theatre, neither of which have much to do with the business presentations I give. Yet they allow me to explore new ways of communicating with people that I can then bring back to my job as a keynote speaker. Without

the Future-Ready Mindset, I wouldn't be so keen to try new things and hunt for learning in unusual places.

What I'm really showing you in these pages is how to take control of your future by creating it, not waiting for someone to decide it for you. If you could do one thing today after reading this chapter, I'd urge you to recognise that what *got* you here won't *keep* you here. You must aim to keep learning, so you can keep *keeping* up! It's vital to success in every field of employment today. You must recognise the need to keep up, not give up, and accept that your future is in your control. No one else can shape it for the better as well as you.

However long you choose to be in the workforce, be that decades or just a few more years, you want to feel useful and valuable in your work, as well as in society and the community you are a part of. It's not just about surviving another workday or workweek, but thriving and loving what you do, proud in the knowledge that you are earning your success in the service of others.

I hope that by teaching you the Future-Ready Mindset, you'll fall in love with exploring new possibilities with eager curiosity, playful creativity, and clear communication with your colleagues. Whether you're in the workforce or an independent professional looking to collaborate with more clients, and business partners, the Future-Ready Mindset is for you.

HAPPINESS ASSESSMENT

Before we go further, you may find it helpful to spend a few minutes reflecting on what makes you happy in your life, and how you feel about change and uncertainty. These seven questions will help you lay the foundations for your Future-Ready Mindset:

1. Be honest, how happy are you with life right now? Give yourself a mark out of ten.

   _____

   _____

2. What makes you happy in your life?

   _____

   _____

3. And what makes you happy when you're working?

   _____

   _____

4. How do you feel about change? Do you always welcome it or sometimes wish you could avoid it?

   _____

   _____

5. If you could choose, would you like more or less change in your life?

   _____

   _____

6. How do you feel when things are uncertain and you are unsure how they may pan out?

_____

_____

7. Would your future be happier with more or less uncertainty and change?

_____

_____

CHAPTER 3

(RE)SET YOUR WAYS

Through my work at Kimberly-Clark and Microsoft and consulting with hundreds of companies, I've been able to hone the Future-Ready Mindset for every personality. No matter your goals or where you are in your career, you can find a way to make this method work for you. Workplace change can be very complex and only you know the exact set of circumstances of your environment. Your working life may be in a constant state of change and turmoil, or it may be dominated by widespread, culturally-entrenched resistance to change. Whatever your situation, you can adapt this process to make it work for you. But that's the bit you'll have to figure out for yourself.

That's why the one thing I tell all my clients is: 'You have to put in the work!' The Future-Ready Mindset process will give you the key steps to follow, but you will need to think carefully about how best to deploy them into your work and life. As long as you respect the order of the steps and put in the effort to work through each in turn, you are sure to get value from the process. However, you should also think carefully about what will work best for your company or organisation. Perhaps your colleagues might respond well to some things and not to others; it's your job to figure out how best to deploy this process into your world of work.

Maybe you're now thinking, 'I haven't got time for this. I'm already busy.' But stop, let's think this through. Part of your 'busy-ness' may be because you haven't stopped to reflect on how to be more productive. Instead of resigning yourself to always being busy or using this as an excuse, ask yourself: 'How can I make the time to become more innovative and ready for change?' We can all make time when we prioritise things sensibly. If the building was on fire, you'd make time to get out, right? Of course!

Exploring the Future-Ready Mindset process through self-reflection and introspection will allow you to pause and make smart changes that will benefit your long-term future. That's why I've come up with this Future-Ready assessment—to get you on the path to resetting your thought patterns. It includes a scenario to think about and an exercise for you to complete—or at least start thinking about. Bonus points if you use a pen and paper, or whatever you prefer to capture notes with.

Assessment #1: What's not working anymore? Think about something that you do at work that's not serving you as well as it might. It might be a regular process, a pattern of meetings, or simply your commute. Could you do it a bit less? Or even stop it completely? Very simply, what can you reasonably **stop** doing? Time isn't elastic—try to do everything, and you'll burn out. You need to make time to allow new things to enter your life and that may mean reducing or completely dropping something you already do. Perhaps you're feeling busy because you're fighting to stay today-ready, not making time for the more important work needed to become future-ready.

Exercise #1: Write down three things that you could perhaps do less often, or stop doing altogether at work. Be brisk with these answers. Don't think too deeply, just write down what comes to mind. (Examples to get you started: Which regular meetings could I reasonably not attend? What's the downside of not getting to inbox zero every Friday? Could I delegate some of my work or use an AI Assistant? Would I benefit from scheduling some quiet time each day instead of simply racing from one appointment to the next?)

Assessment #2: Your current way of thinking. Perhaps you think: 'I'm OK the way I am. I can manage.' Even if you're OK with the way things are, you probably won't get to keep the status quo because more change is coming, no matter what. The one certainty is that change of some sort is never far away, you just don't know when it will strike. Instead of being pleased with how things are, think about how you can make them even better in the future. As I outlined in Chapter 2, what got you here won't get you to where you need to be. If you simply carry on, you almost certainly won't continue to get the same results. If you want your future to be as great as it can be, you have to be prepared to challenge your current ways of thinking and doing. It may feel uncomfortable accepting that you must continue to change and improve forever. This process requires personal reflection, self-awareness, and some courage. If you're relying on your work colleagues to come up with all the ideas that will determine your future, you've put their future ahead of your own.

Exercise #2: How do you cope with change? Think about how your job was five to ten years ago. Have your responsibilities and duties changed or stayed the same? Make a note of some of the significant things you have changed in your approach to work compared to a few years ago. How much has changed, and what role have you played in the past?

Assessment #3: Your comfort zone. The most common objection I get after a talk is, 'My company/boss/team/cat isn't great at embracing new ideas. They don't listen to me, they're not open to change. What's the point? How can I do all this with their negativity?' Don't assume that just because your work colleagues haven't been open to ideas in the past they won't be open to them in the future. Sure, it may seem like they're stuck in a rut following a well-worn path, but if you give them a chance, they may turn out to be amazing at change. You can provide the push that brings their enthusiasm to the surface.

Change is also best when it's incremental, not dramatic. American researcher and scientist Roy Amara found that people routinely overestimate the short-term effect of technology, and yet underestimate its long-term effect. This reminds me of my time at Microsoft when we were sometimes too eager to invest in a short-term, seemingly transformative idea, when what we really needed was consistency and long-term thinking. As individuals, many of us get excited when we get a new smartphone or gadget, but that one device doesn't radically transform our lives. However, over the long-term, the proliferation of smartphones has profoundly changed us as a species and the world we live in.

Exercise #3: What percentage of a typical working day do you spend in your comfort zone? How much time do you spend doing familiar tasks, where you feel relatively at ease and unchallenged? If you say your boss or company isn't open to change, is it really them or you who isn't ready? Do you ever delay change by saying, 'I'll improve this next year when we have the new IT system/ more budget/sunnier weather?' When do you think is really the right time to start?

Assessment #4: The 'Next' Normal. People may say, 'I'd rather have certainty about what I'm doing now than uncertainty and anxiety about the future.' Well, I suspect this is just another creative way of sticking your head in the sand. You need to accept that, for change to happen, you have to be prepared to travel from today and into the unknown, potentially traversing some uncertainty. If you do that, you can get ahead of yourself and find out what new possibilities there are.

Exercise #4: In my talks, I like to show a picture of somebody jumping across a gap—an easy gap—that represents the process of making a change in life. On one side of the gap is the relative safety and familiarity of the place you already know, but there's something on the other side that is uncertain and unknown. You're not sure if you should make the leap or not because the change feels risky, not the jump itself. Ask yourself: What happens if I hop over that gap and make a change? What's the worst that could happen? More importantly, what might happen if I _don't_ jump over that gap? Keep in mind, very few changes in life are truly risky. There's a massive difference between scary and dangerous. Most decisions we're making in the workplace are a little scary at worst. There's very little actual danger involved, and it is highly unlikely that anyone will die from changing the way you organise your team meetings. By understanding the difference between scary and dangerous, you'll recognise how little is at stake in many work-related decisions. So, make the leap, and even if your leap doesn't quite go to plan, at least you've learned how you could leap differently in the future. Without taking the leap, you're guaranteed to learn nothing, stuck in the same place while the world changes around you.

Assessment #5: Happiness after work. If you feel like you don't want things to change in your job, this next assessment will rate your true happiness levels.

Exercise #5: Let's say you're 'comfortable' in your job. But what do you say to others about your job when they ask? Do the pressures of work permeate into your private life? Do you find yourself complaining to friends and family about work or describing your job in a negative way? How content and in control of your work and future do you really feel? Are you truly 'comfortable' in your job?

Assessment #6: The reactions of your colleagues. Let's say the first assessments and exercises are really working for you. Now, what will your co-workers think of your emerging new mindset and enthusiasm for the future? If you discover your passion and excitement for change and suddenly start bringing that energy and positivity to work each day, they may think you've morphed into a different person! Is that too crazy? I'd say it's more crazy to imagine you should stay the same. As you grow in confidence throughout this book, you'll begin to feel more comfortable involving others in your process at a time that's right for you. Plus, if you're toiling away for a change-averse employer who might sack you on the spot just for having an idea, that may be your sign to leave. When you step up and become the driver of change, you have to expect some level of negativity and scepticism from others. But if you stick at it, with time, you'll start to make a positive difference across the organisation, inspiring others to join in with their own ideas and contributions.

Exercise #6: Imagine you present your ideas for some possible workplace improvements to your colleagues. What's the worst thing that could happen? What do you really have to lose? Do your colleagues ever talk or complain about the same issues that you're bringing up? How might they react if you become a driver of change, a bringer of positive momentum? What's worse: sharing some ideas for improvements or sitting back and unhappily tolerating the suboptimal?

Next Steps

As you begin to confront uncertainty, as you just did in these assessments, you're starting to explore the immense value of positive change. You're already becoming more likely to make the leap away from a place of familiarity and complacency into a new world of fresh possibilities for growth. You'll start yearning for the potential benefits of a novel approach rather than catastrophising over unlikely, improbable downsides.

When you have an unshakable Future-Ready Mindset, you'll gladly hop over that proverbial gap any time, knowing the real danger lies in trying to stay where you are.

CHAPTER 4

UNCOVERING YOUR PERSONAL MISSION

The Future-Ready Mindset is rarely taught in business schools or company training programmes. One of the reasons for this is it's a new skill that we didn't need in the past, because our working lives simply didn't change so quickly. The other reason is because this skill melds the personal with the professional. More specifically, the Future-Ready Mindset revolves around your own Personal Mission, which is unique to you and only partially influenced by your own work. It's something you can't really teach, but feel. It's something you nurture from within, but that also has the power to become contagious among your colleagues.

But why is a Personal Mission so vitally important if you wish to develop a Future-Ready Mindset? I don't believe anyone has ever created an amazing future for themselves without first having a reason to do so. If you want to create a brighter future for yourself and those who depend upon you, you must have a compelling motivation—that's your Personal Mission. Without one, you may drift along in life, lacking the drive to seize new opportunities and put in the extra effort needed to improve things at work.

Let's imagine you are a real estate agent, helping property owners find buyers. You might think that your job is to convince homeowners to appoint you to promote their property to suitable buyers so you can bring them a quick, painless, and profitable sale. And if someone asked you what you do for a living, you'd probably say you're a real estate agent, or maybe that you help buyers find the right property for their needs. But there's a problem with this world view; it makes you no different to every other real estate agent, nor does it give you a compelling motivation to continually look for ways you could do your job even better in the future. You're simply selling properties, one every few days, and that's what you're going to do for the rest of your working life.

If you'd like to create an amazing future for yourself, you need a powerful reason to do that. You need to identify with something that's bigger than your job title, more compelling than your job definition, and unique to who you are and the positive difference you make in the world. So, what might your Personal Mission be? You're already great at selling properties, one of the best, but what is it about the work you do that really fires you up and gets you excited? What makes you most proud in your working life that might inspire you to keep wanting to do it better and better long into the future?

Now let's imagine, for example, that you take special pride in helping young adults to find a home where they can settle down and start a family. While your estate agency role may be largely limited to guiding them through their property search, the downstream consequences of doing a great job could be profound. Once settled into their new home, the owners might find great jobs in the local area, build friendship groups, decide to get married, and have or adopt children. Those children may grow up to be the next generation of football or tennis players at the local club, they may one day graduate from college, even work as real estate agents themselves. While it may seem a bit of a stretch from your initial responsibility to help sell a property, it's inescapably true that many of the subsequent events might not have happened without your early involvement helping some young adults find a place they can call home. And if you feel pride in knowing that lives will be better thanks to you, this could provide the seeds for your Personal Mission at work. Instead of saying 'I sell houses', your Personal Mission would inspire you to say, 'I create happy families'.

In identifying an inspiring Personal Mission for yourself you now have a powerful motivator to keep doing what you do and to constantly look for ways you could do it better. Having a focus on young people doesn't prevent you from, say, helping someone to find their perfect retirement home, but it does allow you to concentrate your future focus primarily onto something that feels truly important to you.

In brief, knowing and pursuing your Personal Mission, the higher reason why you do the work you do in the service of others, will give you energy you'll need to keep pursuing positive improvements into the future. Without it, you'll just be doing a job, maybe doing well for yourself, or maybe living from payday to payday, but unlikely to be sufficiently motivated to keep pursuing continuous positive change. You cannot be committed to both your Personal Mission and your comfort zone. Something has to give!

You can think of your Personal Mission as the North Star of your future: It's always there, guiding you, shining down through every challenge, every question, and every task you take on. It will challenge you each day to keep going, to make positive changes, to make lifetime learning and growth a necessity. And once you identify and embrace your Personal Mission, you can easily check in on your progress, asking yourself whether what you're currently working on is serving it well. If a task is an unhelpful distraction, your Personal Mission can help point you towards what might be better ways of spending your time.

In fact, a Personal Mission is so important that it's at the centre of my framework for success and happiness. It's the one thing to focus on if you stripped away all other elements.

There are two key aspects to any Personal Mission:

1. It's something significant you personally care about and want to improve in some way.

2. It's related to the work you're employed to do. It's not a random mission, i.e. you're not going to run off and teach bowling pin juggling to children in Australia if you're a certified bookkeeper for a management company in New York. Your Personal Mission has to make sense for your work. Remember, you need to think of it this way: Your company doesn't employ you to do a job; you employ your company to achieve your potential. Your job gives you an opportunity to shape the world. So, what do you care most about achieving in your work? What will you feel proud of when you achieve it? What will you one day say when your grandchildren or friends or anyone who shows interest ask what you *used* to do when you were working? With a Personal Mission, you won't simply list off your job titles and companies, you'll regale others with fantastic memories of how you changed the world!

Within the boundaries of your job, how can you make the world a better place? Challenge yourself to see if there's something meaningful in your work that you care about more than anything else and want to pursue. For example, you might be employed at a professional cleaning company where you or your colleagues tidy up school classrooms. It may just seem like you're washing floors and putting away things, but your impact is much bigger than that. When you think more deeply about it, you're setting up a classroom for the teachers and students who pass through its doors.

You're preparing teachers for a productive, rewarding day. You're creating a safe, happy place for the next generation of astronauts or accountants or actors. You're preparing everyone for a fabulous day of learning, great weeks, great months, and even great years. Try to connect with that level of meaning in your job. That could be your Personal Mission: 'I give the next generation the best possible shot in life.'

For me, knowing and acknowledging the scale of my Personal Mission has been a driving force to keep me motivated in my work. I want everyone to enjoy the bright future they deserve, which is why my Personal Mission is: "I make people future-ready for life". On the roller coaster ride of getting to know each new client and planning each speaking engagement and project, I return to my Personal Mission. You can do the same. Check in with yourself: Why am I doing this? What do I care most about? How is today's task helping me make the world a better place tomorrow? What's my principal motivation here and who am I working in the service of?

The answer to all of these questions should be found entwined in your Personal Mission, and will be a source of strength to you in the face of the knockbacks or negativity you will most certainly face. Putting yourself out there will always bring out the detractors. Holding a compelling and inspiring Personal Mission in your heart and mind will help you stay strong in the face of whatever challenges life may throw at you.

There are vast cultural and societal differences around the world, and the idea of having a Personal Mission may strike you as entirely sensible or utterly absurd! In the UK, many people tell me they find it embarrassing to say they have a bold or ambitious sense of purpose, while in the USA fewer people have these anxieties. If embracing a Personal Mission feels a bit weird to you, that's fine. In fact, if it doesn't feel a little cringeworthy, perhaps you're not being ambitious enough. Embrace the cringe!

In later chapters, you'll go through each phase of the ReadyAlready Growth Cycle. For now, let's delve into the eight Major Questions you may be asking yourself as you prepare to shape your Future-Ready Mindset. As you're starting to see, though, this mindset is truly a must-have for long-term success when it comes to your future work.

Question #1: Why do I need a process to help me navigate the future?

I mean this in the nicest way possible: You're not the new 'kid' on the block anymore. You've been there, done that, and are looking for more. What got you to where you are may have worked then, but the next steps on your career journey may look very different. In short, you have to keep bringing something new to the party. The Future-Ready Mindset is there to help you maintain your discipline and focus, while your Personal Mission is the North Star that guides you through each part of the process. When you have this structure, you have a compelling reason not just to start, but to keep going, even when the going gets tough.

Question #2: Other people seem to be doing OK. Why do I need a different approach?

Ask yourself, 'Are other people really doing OK?' Are they confident about the future or just getting by? The consulting firm Gartner ran a study where people were asked how well prepared they feel for the future. The vast majority, seventy per cent of people, said they don't feel prepared for the future of work[1], citing lack of knowledge, skills, and even ideas to thrive in the world we have today, let alone the future. Most people, when they think about it, realise it's increasingly hard to make sense of the working world and stay on top. Every day is a struggle and it's sometimes hard to project more than a few weeks into the future.

This is why *you* need a different approach. Your Personal Mission will give you a compelling incentive to keep up and create the future, so you can leap ahead of the seventy per cent of people who are stuck in a cycle of anxiety and worry. With this approach, you'll be someone who's doing something about it and taking the first steps to having greater agency and control over your future.

Question #3: So, what makes this process so special?

To help future-focused people like you, I've codified the

---

[1] Article in Forbes.com. Tracy Bower, PhD: https://www.forbes.com/sites/tracybrower/2022/11/06/70-arent-prepared-for-the-future-of-work-demands-for-upskilling-surge/

most important skills that my team and I (at Microsoft) had to develop so that we could keep up and continually embrace useful change. In the tech industry, we work at the 'bleeding edge' of innovation, constantly buffeting against the winds of change and all its moving parts. My process will help you develop the most vital skills and habits needed to thrive in a world of constant change. At the heart of it, your Personal Mission will keep you hungry and motivated to enhance your future. I've made it accessible with simple, memorable steps that you can truly retain in your mind.

Question #4: Do I have to do everything? Is there a shortcut?

Well, you can pick and choose the path through the processes that work best for you, but I strongly recommend trying to do the whole thing a couple of times first. You may find certain steps more helpful or insightful than others. You may have a preference for communication or creativity or learning. Simply put, you have to work on that for yourself. Remember, though, there's one bit that's utterly essential: Personal Mission. You can't escape that. Without it, you won't get as much benefit from your Future-Ready Mindset as you deserve.

Question #5: Does this work for everyone?

Honestly, I don't know everyone. You, dear reader, are already ahead of most people because you are reading this book. Having said that, the Future-Ready Mindset is universally applicable and has been tried by thousands of professionals in a wide variety of industries and organisations around the world. The beauty is that it contains only the most vital steps—there's no padding or fluff to slow you down—and can be adjusted to your specific needs.

Question #6: What if I just really hate my job?

Let's take a step back: Do you *really* hate your job? Or have you fallen out of love with it and need a new spark? Put aside all the office politics, the people, your boss's annoying habit of clicking their pen during meetings etc. Question whether you *really* hate your job. If you truly do, you're the only person who can change that. Maybe you can use this process to reinvigorate yourself and enjoy a job where you'll feel more inspired and excited about the future.

Question #7: What if I get stuck in the process?

We all get stuck sometimes. Take it step by step and take as much time as you need to think and process the information that you're working through. If you're feeling like it's not working, you may have skipped over something or rushed the process. Follow each section, one chapter at a time, until you feel you know the process well.

Question #8: How do I get my colleagues to do this with me?

Once you've done your inner exploratory work, like finding your Personal Mission, you'll be ready to bring your colleagues in on it. In the TELL step at the end of the ReadyAlready Growth Cycle, the goal is to get your co-workers excited about what you've been doing, so you can get their input, ideas, and support. That's when you'll help them get pumped up for the future and benefit most from their involvement. As a collective, you'll become unstoppable—and will inspire others far beyond your company's walls. But that's all for later. Let's focus on you first, then we'll bring your colleagues into the loop later. Don't try to run before you can walk!

If we're looking at the world at large, the urgent need for enthusiastic people with a Future-Ready Mindset can be found everywhere. Businesses are embracing new technologies more rapidly and with more ambition and confidence. As companies experience the dramatic effect of exponential change brought about by technological progress, they're looking for ambitious, motivated people who can come on that journey with them. When you have these skills, you'll be knocking on an open door to the future.

Businesses that do great things are driven by a collective sense of purpose that supports the individual Personal Mission of each person in the organisation. This is your opportunity to shape what your organisation is trying to achieve.

In the face of so much change, lots of people are struggling to keep up—and are often fearful of the future. As we encounter accelerated change and the growing pressure to learn new skills, employees must have the courage to speak up if they are to reinvent themselves, and leaders need the patience to listen and support. That's why there's a pressing need for a new way of thinking. Sometimes you need to slow down to speed up. And later in your career, it can feel difficult to reinvent yourself.

Coming back to Personal Mission: You can be motivated beyond merely keeping up. You can be driven by a sense of unleashing your genius onto the world through improvements, however minor, that other people will welcome. After all, we are truly working in the service of others in every profession. If you think you're not, what are you doing? Imagine if you could wake up each day with the excitement of knowing you are making the world a better place, not with a sense of resignation or a heavy sigh that says, 'Here we go again'.

We're privileged to be living through a remarkable period of enlightenment. More people are embracing diversity and welcoming uniqueness into the workforce. Sure, we could be cynical and say this is because switched-on companies now identify how beneficial and profitable these characteristics can be. But, as the world has become more diverse, smart companies have kept pace. I encourage you to embrace this opportunity. Your difference and uniqueness, when fully and confidently expressed, can become invaluable to your current job and to your company. You'll come up with new ideas with the right intentions, and spot improvements that will keep the company innovating and delivering better solutions for your customers. Your difference could be tomorrow's brilliance.

So now I hope you can see the importance of having a Personal Mission, which will spur you on and act as your port in any storm. Armed with a passion to make a meaningful difference, you will be energised to keep innovating while also earning the support of your colleagues and bosses. Your values and sense of purpose will help you create better solutions that are profitable and sustainable. Now that's something you may very well teach in your very own class on business someday, but it all started here.

Table: Matching Jobs with Your Personal Mission—Some Examples:

Here are some examples to inspire your own Personal Mission. For each job role example in the table below, the first statement (in **bold**) is a short, punchy, and powerful Personal Mission that you might carry in your mind and share with others. Each following statement (in *italics*) is an optional extra that provides some additional context and justification about how your approach is distinctive and helpful to others. Remember, these are just examples, and your Personal Mission can be as unique to you as you are to the world.

Job	Personal Mission Example
Retail Assistant	**'I give busy people a moment to smile each day.'** *by creating a distinctive shopping environment that's perfect for them*
Health and Safety Officer	**'I make the future better than it would otherwise be.'** *by eliminating workplace injuries and ensuring everyone can look forward to another safe day at work*
Florist	**'I show people they are loved.'** *by creating unique seasonal floral bouquets for all of life's special moments*

Barista	**'I energise city workers so they make smarter decisions.'** *by creating a modern, calming space near their workplace where they can think and recharge*
Accountant	**'I inspire business people to follow their dreams.'** *by providing future-focused financial advice and enthusiastic encouragement and support for ambitious entrepreneurs*
Farmer	**'I give local children healthy eating habits for life.'** *by growing and harvesting the tastiest local, organic produce, so schools can make lunchtime more fun*

Use this space to jot down some thoughts about what your Personal Mission could be. **What do you do in the service of others? How are you changing the world, one working day at a time?**

Remember, your Personal Mission is something that you feel personally invested in and is related to your work in some way. Finding your Personal Mission can be tricky and take time, so use this space to jot down a few ideas, whatever comes to your mind, so you can revisit these thoughts later. The best way to start—and really own—your Personal Mission is with the word "I ..."

CHAPTER 5

THE MISSING PIECE OF YOUR PERSONAL MISSION

I dentifying and adopting a Personal Mission is critical to your success. However, it cannot be the only piece of the puzzle. **In fact, a Personal Mission without direction will leave you lost at sea without a rudder.**

Here's why.

The fundamental problem with how others typically use their Personal Mission is that they focus on how it applies to them right *now*. They focus on whatever's right in front of them—on their day-to-day activities at work. They apply their passion and drive only for the present-day reality instead of stretching it to be focused on success a few months or even a few years from today. Their Personal Mission serves as a compelling motivation to do their job well, but it won't move the needle much unless they're also heading in the right direction. It's a little like the old sports saying: Don't run to where the ball *is*, run to where the ball is *going*.

What you need to do is consider your Personal Mission as an inspiring guide to your desired future state, not simply as a statement of what you do today. And that future state might only be achieved many months or even years from now. Imagine the power of your passion and energy when you apply them to shaping your mid-to-long-term future. Drive + Direction = incredible results down the line.

So, what are others doing wrong? I can break it down into two subsets:

1. **They don't have a Personal Mission at all.** In fact, they may have resigned themselves to doing a job because it pays the bills instead of believing in themselves and working passionately in the service of others. When you don't know the value you bring to the world, you're trapping yourself in a career death spiral.

2. **They have a 'faux' Personal Mission or borrowed one from someone else.** Perhaps the boss, who excels at robotically repeating the company mission statement, told them what their Personal Mission ought to be. Blindly toeing the company line is no substitute for becoming personally invested. Rather than truly feeling their drive, some people pretend to care and are simply going through the motions. As an example, suppose you work in customer service and get caught up on the short-term goals of your immediate environment. In this scenario, you may make the mistake of assuming your Personal Mission

is to answer more calls each day or to get a higher feedback score from each call. You may still be great at customer service, but you need to be more emotionally invested if you are to have great ideas and spot opportunities for improvement that no one else sees. To find the energy to put in the hard yards to make bold changes a reality, you need to live in the service of a meaningful Personal Mission that you truly believe in.

The number one issue with adopting a Personal Mission is that it can be hard to pin down. It may feel very conceptual at first, particularly if you haven't felt that passionate in your work recently. A lot of us go into the job interview feeling like we want to be part of a greater whole, only to get knocked down a few days after picking up our employee name badge. We become immersed in 'all the crazy', the daily grind of how stuff gets done in the company. Work becomes less meaningful, even confusing or conflicting. What was supposed to be a grand part of your career suddenly feels like a tortuous day job. You may lose contact with your original drive, resigning yourself to being a cog in the machine and powerless to change anything for the better.

Your Personal Mission is even harder to maintain when you're constantly being pulled in different directions. The boss may tell you what to do or not to do, while job and career growth opportunities may come and go. Against this backdrop, you can be forgiven for losing your confidence and mojo. At times, as I have during periods of my working life, you may wonder what it must feel like not to be torn apart by anxiety and dread. One sarcastic comment from a colleague or a supervisor may crush your self-belief and enthusiasm.

These are all situations you may come up against and that's why it helps to remind yourself repeatedly of your Personal Mission and how it helps you make a positive difference to the world. Instead of saying you work in the accounting department of a company that makes widgets, remember that people use those widgets to solve their problems—maybe even realise their own life dreams. The more you think about the bigger picture of what you do, the less your Personal Mission will feel like an abstract concept. And the more potent it will become as the energy to inspire your future.

I'll give you my own example of seeing the broader benefits of having a Personal Mission: When I first arrived at Microsoft, the higher-ups put me in charge of marketing for the company's email products. The products in my portfolio were Outlook and Exchange Server (the technical backend of Outlook). In the beginning, I was disappointed since I'd hoped to work on something 'cool and sexy' like Xbox or smartphones. But no, I got email. This felt rather demoralising *until* I realised that every company and every government runs on email. And I now had the world's most used email product as my plaything! My day job was to encourage companies to upgrade their software to get the bells and whistles in the newest version of the software, but my Personal Mission was much more exciting!

I realised I had an opportunity to make the world better at email. I figured, if I could make one per cent of email users one per cent better at using email, the productivity benefits for planet Earth would be huge. Think about it: Billions of people check their email every day but very few do so efficiently and productively. Plus, everyone hates email, but I knew that I could make it fun! With my Personal Mission came my direction, which was to help Microsoft sell millions of upgrade licenses to businesses by making the world better at email every day. I did this by sharing my passion for email productivity in online posts, talking at events, and telling anyone who would listen about the amazing things you could do with email. Making even just a few people better at using email could equate to a significant improvement in productivity for planet Earth. With that clarity of direction ringing in my mind, I used to leap out of bed each Monday morning, excited to pursue my Personal Mission: 'I make the world better at email!' Perhaps adopting your own Personal Mission could give your career a fresh injection of direction and inspire you with the positive momentum you need to create the bright future you deserve.

The Personal Mission is at the heart of a Future-Ready Mindset. It's not a separate thing. It's the guiding light that gives you the energy to create a better future for yourself and others by maximising your chances of achieving the goal within it. And, as you'll soon see, your Personal Mission helps anchor your focus as you work through the simple, repeatable steps in the ReadyAlready Growth Cycle.

Not only will you achieve something special that you believe in, but you're also going to add value for yourself, your company, and the many people you serve. That's why you need the whole Future-Ready Mindset process, not just a compelling Personal Mission. The Personal Mission puts the fuel in your tank. The rest of the steps will propel you forward. Together, they'll give you the courage to think and act differently and, I hope, make improvements to your life, whether big or small. This may seem like a complicated or daunting task at first, but when you start putting your new Future-Ready Mindset into action, you'll quickly realise how having a Personal Mission is helping you create a remarkable tomorrow filled with exciting possibilities.

Use this space to revisit the Personal Mission you started developing at the end of the previous chapter. **Does your Personal Mission still fire you up for the future? Is it focused on a desired future state that will give your career the direction it needs to succeed?**

Spend a little time reflecting on your Personal Mission and making sure it contains enough motivation and ambition to inspire you to pursue it. Don't worry if it feels a little grandiose or overstated, or that you might feel embarrassed sharing this with a colleague. A great Personal Mission is all about you and your future, so get it right for

you and we'll explore how to transform this into concrete
action later in the book.

Part 2

LET'S GET READYALREADY

CHAPTER 6

THE READYALREADY GROWTH
CYCLE EXPLAINED

As we prepare to dive deeper into your Future-Ready Mindset, I want to underscore the significance and uniqueness of the process you are about to discover: The ReadyAlready Growth Cycle.

This framework isn't based on a hard-and-fast formula with dozens of steps or tasks. Instead, it's a simple, practical process for thinking about and creating the future—one that's easy to learn, easy to use, and designed to help you quickly find solutions in your working life. I call it a Growth Cycle because it's a continuous, repeatable process that will help you grow and thrive today and long into the future.

The cycle element of my framework is what really keeps you moving forward and making progress. This unique five-step process—which you'll soon learn in depth—consists of Follow, React, Open, Surprise and Tell (just like my last name, FROST, which I mentioned previously). These five sequential steps will always point you in the right direction no matter where your focus lies or how challenging life may become. In fact, you can follow the process to bring clarity and fresh thinking to any work dilemma or career predicament you face. And it will help put you on a pathway to finding potentially valuable, future-shaping solutions that you can introduce to your work. The best part is, you can master the whole process very quickly, then apply it whenever you need to make sense of something old or new. It contains several vital skills you can apply to your own future, positively influencing your work and life.

The ReadyAlready Growth Cycle is fluff-free, containing only the most crucial concepts you need to transform novelty into opportunity, no matter how your work life may change in the future. Compared to other solutions, it's stripped down to the essentials with minimal steps, so you're less likely to get lost in a complex process. You only need to run through the cycle once to realise how effective it can be to your overall thinking; but you'll love it so much that you'll want to dive in over and over again to extract as much value as you can with each new revolution.

The Growth Cycle is designed to help you identify what matters most to you in the near future. Truly, you can start using it right away, instead of putting it off until that far-away tomorrow we often talk about. With this simple process in mind, you'll quickly understand the process and develop an inspiring Future-Ready Mindset. You'll also be able to discover new things and make yourself indispensable for your company and colleagues. Plus, the more times you work through the cycle, the easier it becomes.

As you continue to develop this mental habit, you'll soon apply it almost instinctively to every challenge you encounter. You'll be able to approach tomorrow with more curiosity, creativity, and courage. The cycle will also exercise your thinking, becoming so ingrained that you'll barely know it's there.

The ReadyAlready Growth Cycle starts by narrowing your focus onto one important *thing*. Our working lives are too often consumed by 'busy-busy' tasks or being pulled in multiple directions. This scattergun approach to work can be very inefficient and tiring as you often end up trying to do lots of things, but none of them exceptionally well. The ReadyAlready Growth Cycle, in contrast, encourages you to focus exclusively on the one *thing* you feel most warm towards—that speaks to you the most loudly—that you believe may have the most potential for your future.

Once you've identified that one *thing*, the process will help you stay focused until you fully understand it and how it could benefit you in the future. The ReadyAlready Growth Cycle is about pursuing a singularity of focus on one goal that supports your Personal Mission while giving you the direction it takes to see it through. (See Chapter 5 for more on Personal Mission coupled with direction as an unbeatable combination.)

Once you embrace the ReadyAlready Growth Cycle, you'll quickly appreciate its simplicity and potential to help you form a new habit, a ritual even, of making conscious, positive choices for your future. Each of the steps opens up countless possibilities, leading you to places where you feel confident enough to excite others about your discoveries so they can help you make your early ideas into an enduring, long-lasting reality.

My best advice is this: Just try it. Give it a go. Take the ReadyAlready Growth Cycle for a spin (pun intended). Bust through any mental objections that may come up, knowing that the benefits will far outweigh the initial learning curve. You'll soon discover the first step can be as simple as writing a to-do list, or even a list of things you 'don't like' about your company and would love to change. Get to step one, and the other steps will naturally follow.

Look, creating a new future can seem daunting without proper direction. Most people drift through life, allowing the tides of change to pull them in whichever direction they are going that day. Consciously creating a future requires a different level of effort and focus. When you use the ReadyAlready Growth Cycle, you'll break a lifetime's habit of waiting to take direction and, instead, do the brave, radical work of listening to your heart and mind, while trusting yourself to set your own direction. This is your opportunity to accept that personal responsibility and start creating a brighter future for yourself and those around you.

You know you need a different approach than other solutions you've tried in the past—and to do that, you must first look inwards. Allow yourself to focus on what makes *you* tick instead of constantly trying to figure out what others want. What's the one success that you'd really love to experience in your work, and how can you make that a reality? The ReadyAlready Growth Cycle will help you understand your inner world, which can then positively enhance the wider world of your colleagues, your bosses, and your customers and all the other people you serve. When you're more in tune with yourself, you'll be able to help more people. You will no longer accept others leading you through life; instead, you'll lead them.

Imagine turning those dull work meetings on their head. Envision yourself playing with ideas that matter to you—that may help improve the world in some way. Making your work life more pleasant and productive is well within your capabilities. The Future-Ready Mindset is a muscle you build by repeatedly working through the ReadyAlready Growth Cycle. Once you've got it, you've got it for life. And on those dark days, where nothing seems to be going right, your now innate levels of curiosity and direction will help you get unstuck every time.

So, what are you waiting for? Let's hop into the ReadyAlready Growth Cycle.

CHAPTER 7

THE NEW HABIT OF A LIFETIME

Now, we've come to the fun part: The ReadyAlready Growth Cycle!

This is a simple, powerful process for preparing you and your organisation for the inevitable changes and challenges of the future—otherwise known as a Future-Ready Mindset. The goal is to get ahead of some of the probable and likely unavoidable changes and challenges of your future working life, rather than allow them to disrupt your plans or drag you in an unexpected direction.

This repeatable cycle is something you can come back to again and again to identify what you should be paying attention to next, so that you can use it to your advantage. This process is centred on your Personal Mission to help ensure you will be making meaningful progress towards a goal that truly matters to you. This motivational focus gives you a clearer sense of how to direct your time and energy onto the most promising opportunities—all to improve your work life. You get to explore your ideas with creativity and curiosity, in ways that others want to, but perhaps lack the process and confidence to do so.

Fundamentally, the outcome that you will get from this process is the confidence to identify new solutions, and to share your discoveries with others to win their support and encouragement. This, in turn, will give you the focus needed to make the improvements a reality. No more grand ideas rattling around in your mind before being forgotten; this is a process that will help you deliver.

You'll surprise yourself and delight your colleagues with renewed self-belief, drive, and passion as you work through this simple process. With the step by step implementation of this system, you'll:

- Channel your energy into what matters most, so you'll feel less randomised in the pursuit of your goals.

- Learn some fun new habits that will help you spot and seize fresh opportunities around you.

- Get better at identifying great opportunities and avoiding the duds.

- Put everything together with clarity, focus, and energy to go the distance.

- Become an agent of change who brings positive improvements to your workplace.

- Play a crucial role in creating the brilliant future that you and your colleagues deserve.

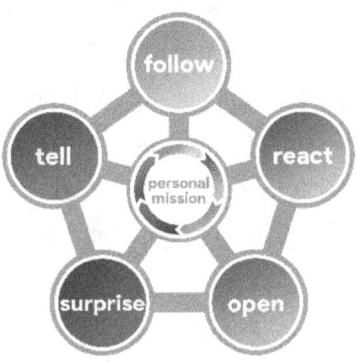

This is the ReadyAlready Growth Cycle. The five steps in this cyclical process are all connected to your Personal Mission in the centre. They are:

- **FOLLOW:** If you're starting this for the very first time, you'll want to identify and narrow down what could be the one *thing* that most deserves your immediate focus. FOLLOW is all about identifying what may matter most in your future, choosing what to ignore, and selecting just one thing to focus on. FOLLOW will help you do one thing well instead of seventy-four things badly!

- **REACT:** In this step, you'll learn all you need to know about your *thing* before choosing your reaction to it. REACT is all about doing careful research on your focus area and finding out all you can so that you'll be able to make better informed decisions. If, after deepening your understanding, you decide your *thing* is still intriguing and likely to be valuable to your future, then you can go on to the next step. If, however, you decide the opposite, that your chosen *thing* is not all that and perhaps not as relevant to your future as first hoped, you can back up to the FOLLOW step and select a different *thing* to focus on. REACT puts you in measured control of your future, making deliberate decisions about what's right for you.

Yes, you are already busy, and it probably feels counterintuitive to elongate the time between discovering something and deciding what to do with it. But, as you'll see, this brief additional pause for thought is vital. You're giving yourself a chance to think and, crucially, a little more time to choose. So often, we want to be the first to do something or to show off what we're thinking to the boss or the team. Instead, when you add in this step, it will ensure that your *thing* has been properly vetted with research and due diligence from you.

A small but important note: Even the most ambitious people may feel tempted to skip the step of REACT—don't be the sort of person who lurches from one idea to the next. That's a disastrous way to find the next big thing. With REACT, you will work smarter and fully explore your *thing* before deciding whether to pursue it for your future.

3. **OPEN:** This step is all about opening your mind to new possibilities. You'll take off the corporate goggles, where the goals of the company are your sole priority, and instead put your Personal Mission first so you can do the best possible work for your company. OPEN

allows you to look at your *thing* with fresh eyes, without the burden of experience. It helps you deepen your understanding by asking simple, naïve questions that others might be afraid to ask. These simple questions might be the ones you have previously hesitated to ask because you were worried that you would look silly. However, by exploring your *thing* with raw human curiosity, you'll begin to see more possibilities for improvements, spot countless quick-win opportunities, and awaken your mind to superior ways to do your work. OPEN is all about looking at the world afresh and exploring the infinite ways that your *thing* could help you achieve more in the future. In a nutshell, OPEN is having the courage and wisdom to question the status quo and create space for easy improvements. Why are things the way they are? Why can't some things be done differently? Why can't you be the person to kickstart the transformation?

4. **SURPRISE:** This step is all about surprising yourself and others with bold, non-obvious, and potentially valuable ideas about how your *thing* may be beneficial to you and your colleagues' collective future. It's about using raw human creativity to dream up new possibilities, have novel, unexpected ideas, and see fresh opportunities. You'll start asking 'What if…?', as you dare to think beyond the obvious. Many people worry that they're not very creative, but when you start having fresh ideas you may find it's strangely

contagious, inspiring your colleagues to also have a go. SURPRISE can help you spot big win opportunities before anyone else, including your competitors.

OPEN and SURPRISE are very similar cognitive tricks that we must play on ourselves to exploit the full capacity of our brains, and see beyond the boundaries set by years of experience. While OPEN is all about looking at your *thing* and naïvely questioning it, SURPRISE is about using your well-rounded understanding of this *thing* to imagine new ways it could benefit your and your company's future.

With SURPRISE, you may start seeing possibilities that you wouldn't otherwise have spotted because it 'wasn't in your job description'. In your creative exploration, you'll have more unexpected and fewer predictable ideas that may eventually prove very useful in the next and final step. You'll be pleasantly surprised with what is possible when you retrain your brain to think differently.

5. **TELL:** This is the vital final step in each spin around the ReadyAlready Growth Cycle where you package up what you've learned and the ideas you're developing. Here, you'll courageously and intentionally tell the right colleagues at work what you've been thinking about, so they can help you improve your ideas and channel them into reality. TELL requires you to show up, open up, and be a little vulnerable. Some of your ideas may be poorly defined, maybe even a bit *out there*. You have to find the courage to lay it

all out to the right colleagues (which we'll identify in more detail in Chapter 12). These friendly colleagues will then, in turn, help make your ideas even more brilliant and actionable.

TELL is where you shift from individual thinking to collective action. You'll choose the right people to confide in; 'who can I work with on this stuff, and what's the right way to do it?' Before the TELL step, you'll want to think about the who, why, and where. The way you TELL is as important as what you're saying. Sure, you could send an email to the whole department, but your idea will most likely die a quick death buried beneath dozens of more urgent emails. Being an agent of change is only possible with the support of colleagues. That's why TELL hinges on intentionally building allies, getting supporters, creating believers, and inspiring them to help you finesse your ideas into a plan that you'll either collectively implement or take to the 'big bosses' to get the resources and support needed to make them a reality.

I mentioned before how the initials of the five outer steps in the ReadyAlready Growth Cycle spell my surname 'FROST'. This isn't because I'm in love with my name and want everyone to know—as a Brit, it actually makes me cringe a bit in embarrassment! The FROST acronym actually came about by accident. But it was a happy accident, because it helps me and you remember the correct order for each of the steps. In the coming chapters, you'll dig into each part of the cycle. And as you go through these steps, you also have free access to some special bonus resources too. Find them at https://ReadyAlready.pro.

Part 3

THE FIVE
FROST STEPS

CHAPTER 8

FOLLOW - FOCUS YOUR ENERGY BY FINDING YOUR *THING*

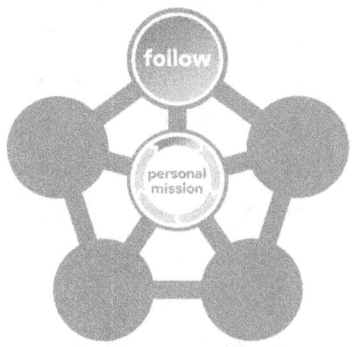

We all have a gap between what we know today and what we may need to know in the future. The gap is ever present, and no matter how much knowledge you accumulate through life, there will always be something new to learn. FOLLOW can help you bridge the gap between who you are today and the person you would like to become. In this step, you will make a list of the things you may need to understand better in the future. Your list might include relatively simple gaps in your knowledge, like figuring out how to use your company's new Staff Leave Booking System so you can look forward to a summer vacation. Or finding an app that can automatically download a podcast series to listen to on the beach.

But it may also contain less obvious things inspired by your imagination of what your future may be. Perhaps you'd like to figure out a way to send order update emails to customers or to reduce your company's carbon footprint by eliminating paper-based processes. Or you might like to know how to outsource repetitive work processes to an outside supplier or find out which software you could use to automate them in-house. Or, you might be curious about how to build a better understanding of advertising regulations, or ways to streamline the company's monthly payroll process. Maybe you'd like to be a more confident presenter, or improve your time management, or simply try out a new bus route for your daily commute. Your future knowledge gaps will be unique to you. That's what makes them so powerful and invaluable for *your* future.

KNOWLEDGE LOADING

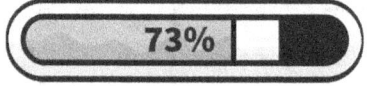

Here's a thought. Wouldn't it be lovely if there was a 'knowledge loading' bar for your life, so you could see exactly how much of all the available useful information you have accumulated, and how much you still have to acquire? You could compare your progress with friends and colleagues, gaining points each time you learned something new. And maybe, with hard work, you could learn more than your co-workers and rightfully be rewarded with the extra pay and perks your learning progress deserves.

Well, sure, that sounds nice, but where would the real fun be in that? Yes, there's a vast amount of stuff that you already know, but seeing the size of the learning task still ahead of you might be truly daunting. Thankfully, there's no such 'knowledge loading' bar and most people are oblivious to how much progress they've made or how much more they still have to learn. And, because of this, many people go through life thinking they have a pretty good handle on most things. Over time, they may even elevate themselves to know-it-all status, the fount of all wisdom for anyone who cares to ask!

But what if you took a different path and revelled in knowing there's always something new to learn? What if you became a learn-it-all?

Wouldn't that make life more interesting and fun? And help you become more ready for the future?

This is the mindset shift you need to embrace in the first step of the ReadyAlready Growth Cycle: **FOLLOW**.

The FOLLOW step is here to help you set the right direction for your Future-Ready Mindset. It also brings the blissful freedom of never having to assume your career goal is to become 'one hundred per cent knowledgeable'. You can leave that sort of madness to the know-it-alls. FOLLOW is the vital first step of our cycle, where you happily accept the limitations of your current knowledge and begin crafting a plan for continuous, incremental development. In this chapter, you'll identify some interesting things you would love to learn more about, including new topics that may help you achieve more in the future. Most importantly, you'll select these topics because you believe they could play an important role in the bright future you will one day enjoy.

FOLLOW is all about finding your focus and identifying the things you need to pay closer attention to now, so you can exploit them in the future to benefit you and your colleagues. Having a Future-Ready Mindset helps you prepare for the inevitable changes and challenges of the future. That word, inevitable, is important. There are many things we may not know much about that are coming at us, whether we like it or not. AI, robotics, self-learning machines, we already know these advances will have a profound, lasting effect on our future lives.

During the FOLLOW step, you will think about what is likely to happen and have a bearing on your working life in the near future. This is not about indulging a wild imagination. It's also not about dreaming up crazy science fiction stuff, but more about dealing with the known realities on your near horizon; one, two, or maybe three years out. In the FOLLOW step, you're going to make a list of everything that comes to mind that you would like to understand more clearly and hopefully be better at in the near future. It can be anything, as long as it relates to your Personal Mission and your work.

Think of it this way: If you're like me, you may get through some parts of your working life bluffing, nodding in meetings, agreeing to things, not really having a deep understanding of what they are, and trying to not look like an idiot by asking daft questions. Having a Future-Ready Mindset is almost the complete opposite. It means being honest with yourself about what you don't know before committing to filling the most important gaps in your knowledge. And this can be a surprisingly hard skill to master! The more senior or experienced you are at work, the more unnerving it can feel to admit that you don't have all the answers. We need to be honest with ourselves. FOLLOW is an exercise in humility and candour, really.

FOLLOW puts you more firmly in charge of your destiny—and it can even feel a little magical to accomplish. Think of FOLLOW as having a mini time machine that gives you a glimpse into your future. With nothing more than your imagination, by squeezing yourself into this tiny time machine, you can be transported a few years into the future, maybe four or five years from now. And when you arrive in that future, you can enjoy a brief glimpse at what your life may become. Peeking excitedly through the windows of your time machine, you realise how different life will be just a few years from today. And, it instantly dawns on you which new skills you'll need to succeed in that future. Now, you can hit the 'TODAY' button on the dashboard of your time machine and return to the present day, with a clear sense of the knowledge and skill gaps you need to fill before you can realise your full potential in the future. That's the stuff to put on your FOLLOW list; all the things that may help you in the near-future.

Activity: FOLLOW

Step 1: Sit down and be ready to write everything out. I'm old-school and love to capture my ideas with pen and paper so I don't get distracted, but do whatever feels most natural to you: type on your smartphone, scrawl on a whiteboard, dictate into a machine, tap on a keyboard. Just be sure to capture *every* thought as it comes to you, no matter how simple, complicated, or weird! Your goal is to create as complete a list as possible, catching every idea you have as you have it. Don't waste time editing your list. That will come later. For now, simply gather as many thoughts as you can; the more, the merrier!

You're looking to make a list of all the things that seem potentially important to your future work that you probably ought to understand better. If you get stuck, think about this: What do you not understand well enough at work today? It might be something simple like figuring out how to do double-sided printing with automatic stapling—a skill I've never mastered but which might be useful for the future. It might be that you would like to have a better understanding of some software, or a process, or a new way of working. Think carefully, and write everything down, no matter how small or trivial. The key insight here is, you don't need to pursue a radical reinvention of yourself. If you're a management accountant, learning how to be an astronaut or physiotherapist is probably a wild stretch from the likely future scope of your work! Any idea that's too big or too complicated will almost certainly be beyond your short-term reach. Keep it realistic; you don't need to reinvent yourself or your company. Look for things within your field of view that you could understand better and potentially have some future influence over. There's a reason most New Year's resolutions fail. 'New year, new me' is too sudden and ambitious, so most people have given up by mid-January. If this has happened in your life, you may not have been sufficiently motivated to see your ambition through. But you are now.

Step 2: Make a list, a long list. Take as long as you need, several days or weeks even, just start making a list of things you would like to know and be better at in the near future. It's the best to-do list ever because it's all about you, what motivates you most, and the topics that may hold the key to your future happiness.

Here's another work-related example: One of the people at my talks, the Chief Finance Officer of a global company, identified that he would love to know how to use Microsoft Excel, the spreadsheet software, better. In thinking about his future, he realised that he had never taken the time to properly understand how to use Excel, and that fixing this gap in his knowledge might be pivotal to his future. Admitting this in front of his deputies took real humility and courage, and I loved his honesty. He was worried that learning Excel was too trivial, too silly, to put on his FOLLOW list. But it was exactly the sort of learning opportunity that could make a huge difference to his future happiness and his prospects at work. Similarly, the items on your list could be very specific job skills like this, or soft skills like time management, presenting, pitching, etc. It doesn't matter what it is, as long as it matters for you and your future work pursuing your Personal Mission.

Remember, you're trying to prepare yourself for the inevitable changes and challenges of the future, so think about the skills and knowledge you may need to have next. The ideas may come to you easily, or you may have to tease them out of your mind with lots of concentration. Some may not feel ambitious enough or particularly future-focused. That's fine, as long as they still feel right for you and your work.

As an example, let's say you work for a company that improves road safety by designing safer street layouts and advising town planners. You love your job, and your Personal Mission is to make roads safer for everyone. As you think about your job, ask yourself: What may be different in the future compared to today? You start jotting down some ideas as they come to mind. For example:

- There will be designated walking and cycling lanes in all densely populated areas

- Smart road surfaces will be equipped with traffic sensors for accident monitoring
- Road visibility will be better with adaptive street lighting and signage
- Variable speed limits will auto-adjust to weather and driving conditions

As you explore these possibilities, you reflect that better road design will be only part of the solution; you will also need drivers to behave more responsibly and for smart vehicles to do more to keep others safe. Today, your job is to design safer road layouts. Vehicle specifications and road regulations are beyond your current remit. But 'future you' may need to know much more, like understanding the capabilities and limitations of self-driving cars and road monitoring technologies. You might add some future concepts to your FOLLOW list:

- Self-driving, fully autonomous vehicles with collision avoidance?

- No speeding with automatic enforcement of variable speed limits via in-vehicle software?

- Children and adults to receive regular road safety education?

- Universal use of front and rear cameras with remote police monitoring?

- Regular re-testing of drivers, maybe every ten years?

- AI-powered systems to detect and penalise unsafe drivers?

You can keep going for as long as you like. This is part-brainstorm, part future projection, but the result is a list of new learning opportunities for you, some of which might ultimately prove hugely important in your career.

Step 3: What's your *thing?* When everything is written down, pick one *thing,* just one. Identify the *thing* on your FOLLOW list that speaks to you most loudly, that would serve your Personal Mission well, and that you simply cannot afford to delay learning about any longer. This will be your *thing,* the one special topic that will be your focus as you work through the rest of the ReadyAlready Growth Cycle.

By writing this list, you're lifting a huge weight off your shoulders by proactively identifying and acknowledging all that you don't yet know. And in committing to focus on just one *thing,* you're moving on from any resistance, denial, and delusion you might have about your abilities, and being brutally honest and realistic in setting one simple priority for your immediate future. Selecting your one *thing* is often quite difficult. But that's the nature of true focus: being able to completely ignore things you would really love to work on to give your full attention to the one *thing* that matters most. Finding your focus in FOLLOW can be both challenging and hugely rewarding.

Now, I want to caution you that it's important to do the steps in their order. Starting with FOLLOW gives you a long list of ideas and possibilities, before you narrow it down to just one *thing*. Your future begins the moment you focus on what's most important to you. Far too often, we're pulled in different directions at work. FOLLOW is the first step you need, where you start taking back control and allowing yourself the time and space to create your future. We start with FOLLOW because it's about reducing the noise and removing the clutter. I personally keep a running FOLLOW list that I can always go back to, and I'm constantly adding and deleting items on my list as my interest in them rises and falls. Your chosen *thing* might seem a bit mundane, or even radically important. It's up to you to decide what most deserves your attention and will inspire you to action.

This is a critical step in the ReadyAlready Growth Cycle. If you get this right, everything else that comes next will be fascinating, fun, and relevant to you. Finding an interesting and worthwhile *thing* to follow is really, really important. But don't stress about it too much. Even if you get it wrong, there's a chance to put things right in the next step in the cycle. So, don't wrap yourself up in anxiety by making this decision more daunting than it needs to be. Instead, compile your list, pick the one thing that's speaking to you most loudly, and we'll validate it in the next step. Take your time, give it your best shot, and just keep reminding yourself that this is an exercise in humility, honesty, and hopefully discovering something new that will help you in the future.

Please remember too that there's no shame in admitting you don't have certain skills or knowledge. In fact, being honest about your limitations is the first step towards future-readiness and can be immensely empowering and uplifting—even cathartic. Being truthful about what you still have to learn is the key to unlocking the future potential that you might otherwise never have unleashed. This mindset shift alone will give you a huge lead over colleagues and competitors who have not yet had this realisation.

Remember, this process is not about proving your genius. It's about proving your current limitations so you can do the work to reduce them. The things that you can deal with are the ones you can fix—you just haven't got around to addressing them *yet*. A lot of the items you add to your list may be relatively new to you because you've only heard about them in the last few weeks or months. This is why I often chat with clients about emerging developments like AI and quantum computing; both are real and fascinating and are likely to transform many jobs for years to come.

The FOLLOW step directly relates to your Personal Mission but gives it a sense of direction. As I've talked about in this book, I developed a passion for email productivity that served me well at Microsoft. It all started with a simple question to myself: What can I do better with email? I then asked more questions about how I could help others be more productive with email. As I and many others who have used this framework did, write your list and just go back and cross-check everything that's there to ensure it supports your Personal Mission in some way. Then, double check: Does this make sense? Might this help me achieve my Personal Mission? Am I heading in the right direction?

You've made your FOLLOW list, and you've picked your one *thing* to focus on. It's now time to get to know your *thing* better. Step two in the ReadyAlready Growth Cycle is REACT, and it's all about new learning and making an important decision for your future. Let's do it!

Reader Recap: FOLLOW.

- **On why we do FOLLOW first.** If you were to try to learn all you need to know about every item on your FOLLOW list from top to bottom right now, you might never finish. Even after tidying up and simplifying your ideas, you may still have an overwhelming number of tasks awaiting your attention. And, as you explore each item, you are likely to uncover yet more ideas to add to your list. The number of hours in each day is stubbornly finite, so you need to be realistic here! Having come this far, you have already proved that you are smart and can do anything, but you can't do everything. So, to fast-track your journey through the ReadyAlready Growth Cycle, you must select just **one** item from your FOLLOW list to work on. This will be your *thing*; the single area of interest that you believe will benefit you most in the future. After you have found your *thing*, you will concentrate solely on this for the rest of this cycle. It's important that you choose with care, so take your time and pick whatever feels most important to you.

- **On why one thing.** Why only *one thing*? Why not two, or more? With a lengthy list of future possibilities, it's easy to become distracted and weighed down by the sense of responsibility. You want to stay in control, not overwhelmed, as you plan for your future. And it's always better to do one thing well than several things badly. Focusing on one learning topic at a time and then exploring it fully will help strengthen your Future-Ready Mindset. And don't worry that by picking only one item, you are leaving good ideas behind. Your FOLLOW list is yours to keep, and you can revisit it on your next spin of the ReadyAlready Growth Cycle.

- **On finding time to plan for the future.** The most common complaint I hear from executives as they work through the ReadyAlready Growth Cycle is not having enough time to plan for their future or to do this extra thinking on top of their day job. On questioning, many report the shortage of time is rarely because of daily work pressures, but more commonly a failure to fully concentrate on one development opportunity at a time. I call this SOS, 'Shiny Object Syndrome', a common affliction which steals our attention and pulls us towards the latest new 'shiny' thing that catches our eye. We don't want to leave opportunities on the table, so we feel we should be on top of everything, and SOS keeps pulling us in new directions. The result is that we may feel paralysed by possibilities or never able to do a thorough job on each available option. With SOS, our understanding of the new remains paper-thin and our progress towards the future can slow to a crawl. The cure for SOS is simple: Focus with FOLLOW.

- **On trying to do it all.** Confucius said, *'the man who chases two rabbits catches neither.'* Instead of trying to do everything on your FOLLOW list, you must focus on the one topic that matters most to you. When you find it, lock onto that one thing and go deep. Pursue it obsessively. Understand it fully. And don't lose focus until you feel you have mastered it completely.

- **On having to choose just 'one *thing*'.** Selecting your *thing* may feel daunting, but you should take comfort from knowing that by picking a favourite, you are not rejecting all the other ideas on your list. You will simply put these to one side while you focus on your chosen *thing*. Electing to ignore opportunities to allow you to excel at another is the pinnacle of focus excellence! And, remember, the next step in the ReadyAlready Growth Cycle, REACT, includes a helpful validation process where you can change your mind and return to the FOLLOW step if needed. This isn't the end of your list, it's simply the beginning.

- **On being honest with yourself.** As you look through your FOLLOW list, be honest. The biggest, most complicated ideas might be the worst place to start putting your Future-Ready Mindset into action.

Something simple, like getting better at the basics of your job, might be a quicker route to success in your career. Don't worry about how others may judge you, and don't stress about getting it wrong. Choose whatever feels right for you. Follow your gut instinct and lock on to your *thing* with enthusiasm and self-belief. You've got this!

Use this page to start jotting down some items for your FOLLOW list. What topics, techniques or skills might you need to understand better in the near future? What new knowledge might help you deal better with some inevitable changes and challenges that lie ahead as you pursue your Personal Mission?

Remember, items in your FOLLOW list can be anything from soft skills like time management to deep knowledge like understanding a new piece of legislation or tax policy. As long as the items on your list are relevant to your work and your near-term success at work, they will be worthy contenders. One of these may even become your *thing*.

Case Study #1: Volvo Engineer Nils Bohlin Changes Seatbelts

Not long ago, even the idea of wearing seatbelts in cars seemed absurd. In 1958, when Nils Bohlin, a Volvo engineer, patented the three-point seatbelt, the New York Times reported it as 'a violation of human rights'. A public health report described the wearing of a seatbelt as 'ineffective, inconvenient, and uncomfortable'. Yet, Volvo persisted, introducing the improved seatbelt to all their vehicles and generously making their patent freely available to other vehicle manufacturers. The three-point seat belt is now fitted as standard in nearly every vehicle on the road today. Nils Bohlin's visionary approach and relentless resolve have saved countless lives.

Having the courage to dream beyond today's reality is a crucial part of the process of developing a Future-Ready Mindset. The reason you will need this bravery is because this isn't a perfect science. Some of your best thoughts may come from your current understanding of the world today. Others may be inspired by something you have seen, imagined, or dreamed about. Never worry if the things you are interested in or the ideas you have seem silly, odd, or even implausible. Wearing a seatbelt in moving vehicles seems eminently sensible today, but this concept once attracted near-universal ridicule. Preparing yourself today for likely future possibilities may just give you the edge you need to leap ahead of your competitors.

As you think about potential future scenarios relating to your work, consider the new skills you may need to make them a reality. Consider this:

- What areas of expertise might you need to develop?
- What learning experiences could be beneficial?
- What skills might I take for granted in the future that I can start developing today?

The Personal Mission you identified earlier will help you stay focused. For a vehicle designer or road safety designer, an ideal future state might be the day when you have done such an excellent job that there are no accidents, no deaths, or even any injuries on the roads. Perfectly safe travel by road; wouldn't that be nice? Try picturing yourself at this future date, when you will have completed everything you set out to achieve. From this future viewpoint, you will reflect on your PERSONAL MISSION with a sense of pride and satisfaction, but also a clear understanding of the learning journey you had to go through to get there. What might 'future-you' understand well that 'present-you' could start learning today?

Case Study #2: One CFO's Hesitation

One of my favourite suggestions for a thing came from a Chief Financial Officer (CFO) of a global company I was working with. He had invited his team of Regional Finance Directors to London, UK, for the company's annual business review and planning sessions. I joined the meeting for a couple of hours to help the team explore ways to improve productivity and streamline their finance processes. I coached the meeting participants to compile their own FOLLOW list, then invited volunteers to share suggestions for what might become their *thing*. Some brave hands went up to offer their ideas with one director talking about wanting to automate her region's accounts payable procedure. Another wanted to improve diversity in his team to meet company targets. Someone was keen to explore how their treasury operations could benefit from cryptocurrencies and blockchain technologies.

From his seat at the back of the room, I could tell the CFO had an idea, but was hesitant to speak up. I asked if he had a *thing* he wanted to share and he replied,

"No, not yet. It's a bit silly really. I'm not sure my idea is right." I reminded him that there are never wrong answers, just promising possibilities to explore. Then, with obvious embarrassment, the CFO said, "OK, could my *thing* be Microsoft Excel? I never learned how to use spreadsheets properly; I'm self-taught. I get some great reports from the team and would like to dive deeper into the numbers. Could Excel be my *thing*?"

It was a mic-drop moment. Without prompting, someone started clapping, then others joined in. This moment of humble honesty from the most senior person in the room was jaw-droppingly powerful. And he was right, at first glance Excel seems a rather basic *thing* to want to know better in the future, especially for a Chief Financial Officer. But if that's the most important item on your FOLLOW list, that's exactly what you should focus on. The CFO's nervousness and disarming honesty delivered a valuable message to everyone in the room that day. It is OK to admit you need to be better at something. It is OK to work on improving yourself. It is OK to be human. In fact, you'll never develop a Future-Ready Mindset unless you're prepared to be honest with yourself and others.

Once you've picked your *thing*, write it in giant letters in your notepad or pin it up by your desk. That's your *thing*, be proud of it! A host of exciting new possibilities awaits.

Congratulations! Step one in the ReadyAlready Growth Cycle is now complete. Give yourself a pat on the back! You've made some valuable discoveries, begun developing some new opportunities for your future, and are already thinking more deeply about how you will realise your full career potential at work. You have also identified a topic that feels important to you and selected it as your *thing*. It may not feel like much, but the process you have gone through could soon bring immeasurable benefits for your future.

Before you move to our next step, there's one extra job you need to do, and this is supremely important. Put your FOLLOW list somewhere safe; you may need it again soon. Store your list in a drawer, save it on your computer, or keep a photo of it on your phone. You don't want to lose any of those interesting observations. The ideas you compiled still hold plenty of promise but, for now, they are not your top priority. That honour goes to your *thing*.

CHAPTER 9

REACT - LEARN, THEN DECIDE

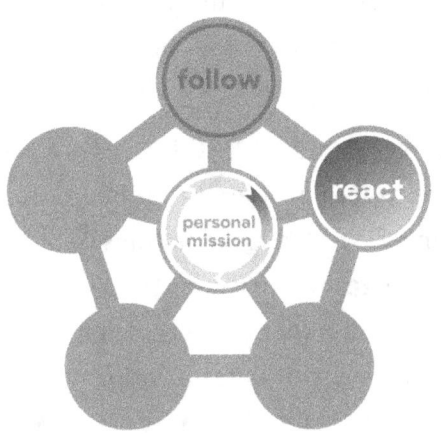

REACT is where you make a wise choice to walk before you run. It is a journey of discovery where you will learn all you need to know about your *thing*, before deciding if it really will be useful to your future. REACT is part-education, part-verification. It's a brief period of validation to ensure the topic you selected in the FOLLOW step is everything it promised to be. In this second phase of the cycle, your reaction will tell you how beneficial your *thing* may be to your future. At the end of this step, you will be ready to make an important decision about whether to explore it further or to focus on something else instead.

REACT is an important part of the process because it buys you a little time to get to know your *thing* properly, before deciding if it's right for you at this moment. It's a lot like dating, really. When meeting a new social contact or potential life partner, it pays to get to know them properly before you inadvertently fall head-over-heels in love with the wrong person. In much the same way, REACT can ensure you do not find yourself locked in a long-term relationship with the wrong *thing*, building a future you may soon regret.

Another reason why REACT is important is because we often race to find answers to problems before properly understanding the full range of options open to us. Imagine if you won a superpower in a competition and had to decide whether you would rather be invisible or have the power to fly? Faced with only two options, most people would have little difficulty choosing which superpower they would prefer. You may even have strong opinions about why one is clearly better than the other. The same efficiency of response governs many other choices we face in daily life. Humans are biologically wired to respond rapidly to 'A or B' choices. This is partially governed by our instinctive fight-or-flight response, a ruthlessly efficient mechanism that helps keep us safe and alive. By compelling us either to put up resistance (fight) or to flee to safety (flight), a speedy response can be a lifesaver in dangerous situations. But this same speed and efficiency can also work against you, compelling you to make snap decisions that may prove detrimental in the longer term.

With your fight-or-flight instinct unconsciously guiding your response, it's natural to assess each new choice you encounter as either having many inherent problems ('this doesn't feel right, I don't like it') or being the best solution you're likely to find, removing the need to evaluate any other possibilities ('that's good enough, let's give it a try'). Either of these snap reactions could prove damaging in the longer term if you don't understand the broader ramifications of your chosen solution. REACT exists to inject some much-needed rationality into your decision-making and help keep you safe from dodgy choices!

Fortunately, evaluating the options for your future will, I hope, be far from a fight-or-flight, life-or-death choice, but you may still be susceptible to reaching a subconsciously biased 'love or hate' verdict. You already know your *thing* is interesting and intriguing—you wouldn't have picked it otherwise!—and you may have an underlying motivation to prove yourself right. This gives you a strong incentive to see the positives in your *thing*, potentially at the expense of not spotting some of the downsides. It's not quite love-at-first-sight, but something inspired you to pick your *thing* above everything else on your FOLLOW list. The flames of interest are already there. So, let's make sure it's right for you before we get in too deep!

I've seen several promising business ideas veer off track at this stage, with teams failing to evaluate properly the pros and cons before leaping into action. Caught in the buzz and positive energy of getting stuff done, they race ahead at full speed, trying to steal a lead over competitors, or attempting to beat their own self-imposed deadlines.

Do you remember when virtual reality (VR) headsets first became affordable? They were the coolest technology gadget in town. Thanks to tiny screens worn over the eyes and the wizardry of software, VR could instantly transport the wearer to a magical virtual world where anything was possible. Business leaders scurried to join the gold rush by incorporating a VR experience into their promotional activities. But, as calmer heads know, becoming hopelessly besotted with an idea can blind you to its potential downsides and weaken your capacity for critical thinking.

Trade shows and exhibitions became an early graveyard for many ill-conceived VR initiatives. If you've ever attended an exhibition, you'll know they can be intensely competitive spaces, with stallholders deploying all kinds of wacky tactics to grab the attention of passers-by. In its early days, VR promised to be a radical differentiator that could showcase how innovative and forward-thinking exhibitors were. I visited trade stands where I wore VR headsets that dropped me into pixelated game environments. I interacted awkwardly with virtual products. And—get this—I even endured a memorably bad demo where the VR experience was limited to looking at a 3D version of the exhibitor's company logo! Hardly the stuff of dreams...

Predictably, most of these VR experiences were profoundly underwhelming. In their haste to try something new and interesting, countless companies fell into the love-at-first-sight trap. Rather than invoking cautious, sceptical curiosity, their response was wild, rampant affection! They threw all their eggs into the VR basket, and the end result was a soggy, scrambled mess! And rather than showcasing these exhibitors as trailblazing VR pioneers, many ended up looking like lazy, unimaginative copycats. In a cruel twist of irony, their quest for novelty and exclusivity had pushed them to replicate the very same mistakes as their competitors.

These days, you're less likely to see ill-conceived VR installations at trade exhibitions and shows. Many of the early adopters have moved on to something new, with memories of their early VR disasters quietly forgotten. Maybe they have found something else that's new and shiny and are giving that a try. And the same mistake will repeat itself, year after year.

If only those early VR experimenters had spent more time understanding their *thing* more completely, checking whether their initial excitement was justified, and adjusting their thinking as their knowledge developed. They should have slowed down, bought themselves some thinking time, and fully explored the many possibilities on the horizon. It's always best to evaluate both the pros and the cons, consider alternatives, and keep learning until you have a well-informed, balanced opinion. Then, and only then, should you decide how to proceed. That's the REACT step in a nutshell.

In REACT, you should learn as much as you can and then determine if your *thing* is still relevant to your future or not. It's about making a commitment to personal growth through learning. How many times have you thought, 'I should listen to that podcast,' so you subscribe, but never get around to playing it? Or maybe you've bought books in the past that, for whatever reasons, you never found time to read? Or have you excitedly signed up for an interesting webinar or online training programme, only for the scheduled time to arrive and you decide you suddenly have something more interesting to do? It's easy to learn these days, but it's even easier to avoid learning. The REACT step will help you sidestep any avoidance tactics you've developed in the past, giving you a compelling reason to do the research, listen to the podcast, and pay full attention in class!

You have your FOLLOW list, you've decided what your *thing* is, so now is your chance to learn all about it once and for all. Very soon, you'll know more about your *thing* than anyone you work with. Perhaps you'll be surprised how a little knowledge can make you an expert amongst your peers! And let's keep things realistic: You don't need to become a world-renowned professor in your *thing*. You just need to know enough to make an informed initial decision about its probable usefulness to your future before you can progress to the next step.

Why is it important to do this step in this order? Many people gloss past the REACT phase, or don't do it at all. They don't take time to learn, to think, or to understand fully. They develop a wafer-thin understanding, knowing just enough to be dangerous, but not enough to do anything to a competent level. That's why REACT can be such a transformative step for people who might otherwise have skipped over it entirely. The reason why you need to do this step right now is to avoid the Shiny Object Syndrome (SOS) trap of naïvely jumping on the first novelty you come across. By building your own familiarity with the subject matter and focusing on what's relevant to you, you'll make better decisions about your *thing*. Trends and fashions belong on the catwalk. What you need is to make sure you have found the right *thing* for you and your Personal Mission.

SOS is a dangerous condition. You'll know you've got it when you find yourself fixating on the novelty of something new rather than exploring the bigger picture of what's most sensible for you right now and in your near future. FOMO, fear of missing out, also plays a role here. For example, when your competitors start posting on a new social media channel, you might feel you need to be there too. But following someone else's bad decision is a terrible basis for setting your future agenda. Do your own research, decide what might be useful, and then fully evaluate it to determine if it's right for you.

REACT is such a crucial step. In the early days of digital transformation at Microsoft, we would try all kinds of things, spending huge amounts of money in the process. Some of it worked, some of it didn't. With hindsight, if we had pursued fewer shiny objects and novelties, we might have achieved more through focus and better discipline. Similarly, what you need to do is to avoid the misery of grabbing onto random new stuff only to abandon those initiatives a few months later. REACT can be your permanent cure for SOS.

Fundamentally, REACT is about getting your head around something seemingly important you didn't previously understand. It affords you the time and space needed to build out your personal knowledge before you can apply the human superpowers that come later in the ReadyAlready Growth Cycle. Ultimately, you'll convert the knowledge you gain here into valuable, non-obvious ideas that others cannot yet see. This is what you're trying to get to, and later on, you'll see how this can help you leap ahead of competitors or introduce groundbreaking thinking at your company.

More than anything, REACT is a learning step, a vital stage of study and education, and you're going to have to do the work. The first small step you can take is this: Think about all the interesting ways you could learn about your *thing*. Your instinct might be to start diving into searching online or asking AI to tell you everything you need to know. But before you do this, ask simply, 'How many different ways could I learn about my *thing*?' There are so many possibilities. You could read a book about it, you could watch online videos, you could attend a webinar, you could ask experts for advice, you could tune into a podcast on the subject, or even go to a conference in your city or a nearby town. You could join a training course or read a research report… There are so many interesting ways to learn these days!

When you've explored all your learning possibilities, start with the one that appeals to you most—a task that you think you'll really enjoy. If you love books, go to a library or bookstore. If you love podcasts, fire up the app and hunt for helpful episodes. Next, commit some quality time to exploring and learning whatever, wherever, whenever you can. The key is to learn enough for your needs, not to burden yourself with trying to know everything.

A little insider's tip: You often don't have to know much about a given topic to know more than your colleagues or boss. Always keep that in mind. Don't feel like you have to become the world's expert in your *thing*. You just need to know enough to make an informed choice at the end of this step.

Importantly, never forget that there will always be more you could learn. When you start using your new knowledge in your work and a question comes up that you don't know the answer to, you can always go back to REACT to learn a little more. But that also doesn't mean you should be lazy and skip over the details in this step. Take your time. Don't rush.

REACT supports your Personal Mission because you're proactively doing something that might help you be successful and achieve more in the service of others. There's never any guarantee that you'll find a silver bullet that will solve all your future problems, but there's always a chance, and that should drive you forward. When you know you're pursuing something relevant and important to your future, any learning task can be inspiring and uplifting. When you're learning, you're growing. You're not simply surviving in the day-to-day, trudging through the treacle of your daily existence, but you're stretching your mind, expanding your comfort zone, and investing in your future potential. You're gathering information that you hope will prove to be valuable. But your starting motivation should be to do something worthwhile just for you. So, if watching a relevant-sounding TV documentary could possibly help you achieve your Personal Mission, you should absolutely sink into a comfortable chair with your favourite beverage. And treat yourself to some popcorn too. You deserve it!

If you've gone this far, you're already well ahead of so many people. Most professionals don't even complete the first two steps of the ReadyAlready Growth Cycle. And if they do, they stop here, having done the bare minimum amount of learning before lurching into the implementation phase. Worse still, if they have SOS, it won't be long before they move on to the next shiny object, then the next, on their hamster wheel of trial and error. You, however, know you have completed just two of the five steps! You have three more steps to get to a level where you can have a fresh, well-rounded perspective, bright new ideas, and the support of your colleagues to lay the foundations for your collective future.

At this point, you may find it feels mentally and even physically rewarding to be finally doing something positive about your future. And you may already feel a small sense of accomplishment. It's good to do something that may be good for you. But you're not there yet! Now is the moment to make a vital decision before continuing.

The REACT step is named this way because it's all about the reaction you have to your *thing* after you've learned about it fully. How will you react to your *thing*? Does it still fill you with interest and hope, or is it starting to feel like a dead end? Is it likely to be useful in your future? Is it worth pursuing further? Or is it a dud, a let-down, a lead balloon?

It's time to decide how to react. If, after careful consideration, you decide you really like your *thing* and want to explore it more deeply, simply move on to the next step, OPEN. If, however, you are feeling like your chosen *thing* is not as exciting or relevant or useful as you initially hoped it might be, you don't have to keep chasing a rainbow! Simply reject your *thing*, then restart your journey through the ReadyAlready Growth Cycle by returning to your FOLLOW list and choosing a new *thing* that sings most loudly to you. And then come back to restart REACT with this new *thing*.

When you eventually have a *thing* that has passed the REACT test with flying colours—whether that's on your 1st or 17th try—I hope you will be buzzing with excitement to explore it further! This is where your journey through the ReadyAlready Growth Cycle really starts to get fascinating. You will soon tap into three remarkable human superpowers to explore your *thing* in a refreshing new light. The coming stages will challenge you to use your curiosity, creativity, and communication skills to uncover new possibilities for your future. Your adventure continues with OPEN, in the next chapter.

Reader Recap and Worksheet: REACT.

- After you've learned all you can about your *thing*, you must choose how you will REACT to it. In simple terms, you need to consider the knowledge you have gained to decide if your *thing* is worth exploring further. If it is, you will continue through the remaining steps of the ReadyAlready Growth Cycle. If it isn't, you will return to the FOLLOW step and start afresh with a new *thing*.

- So, how will you REACT? Do you see future potential in your *thing* or has your burgeoning relationship started to cool?

- This is a crucial part of the Future-Ready Mindset process, calling for a cool, level-headed reaction, not a spur-of-the-moment choice. And that's not always as easy as it sounds. You are probably already emotionally invested in your *thing*. You chose it of your own free will and you may feel compelled to try to prove your initial instinct was right. But you're in a different place now. You've learned all you can about your *thing* and are now seeing it through more experienced eyes and with a broader understanding of its pros and cons.

- Here are some suggestions to help you choose your reaction and decide whether to keep working with your *thing* or to move on to something new. Asking yourself these questions may help focus your mind:
  » Are you still intrigued by the potential of your *thing*?
  » Are you puzzled why your colleagues are not making better use of your *thing*?
  » Can you imagine a future work-related application for your *thing*?
  » Are you eager to tell work colleagues about your *thing* and see what they think?
  » Would you feel frustrated in a month's time if you weren't doing more with your *thing*?

If you find yourself answering 'no' to two or more of these questions, perhaps your *thing* isn't all it was first cracked up to be. If it no longer feels as exciting as first promised or you are sensing more negatives than positives, maybe it's not right for you and your future. Or, perhaps you now see too many potential barriers to success for your *thing*, or you sense its implementation may be more problematic than you first imagined.

- If your reaction is 'NO', it's possible that your *thing* is more of a 'not-now-thing'. As an idea, it may be ahead of, or even past, its time. For whatever reason, it just doesn't feel right for you and your future, and that's fine. Put this idea and any notes you have compiled to one side and return to the list you made during FOLLOW. Pick another *thing* to work on before you start learning afresh with REACT.

- However, if your answer to most of the questions is 'YES', your *thing* clearly shows promise and may one day prove to be valuable to your work and career. By building a solid understanding of your *thing* during REACT, your confidence in its future potential has grown and you are now ready to delve deeper into the unexpected possibilities it may one day bring into your life. No SOS for you, just diligent learning and a well-informed reaction!

Case Study: Microsoft

Early in my career at Microsoft, I discovered the power of continuous learning and expressing a clear opinion. The company's technologies were constantly changing, and simply keeping up with everything new felt like a full-time job. Through some cruel twist of fate, I was put in charge of marketing for one of the company's least exciting technology areas: email. My products were everybody's favourites: Microsoft Outlook and something called Exchange Server that makes the email magic happen behind the scenes. My job was to grow the business by inspiring more organisations to spend big to buy the latest version of our software. As a creative marketing specialist, I felt adrift in an ocean of IT developers. Frankly, I didn't understand email or software nearly as well as my Microsoft colleagues did!

One morning, during our weekly team meeting, my manager mentioned he had heard about a new way of sharing information online. Some of our software developers were now sharing advice online using what my boss called a 'weblog', or 'blog' for short. This struck me as an intriguing way to communicate with people outside of Microsoft and maybe showcase some of the human faces working inside the tech giant. As usual, I scribbled 'Blog?' in my notebook, so that I could investigate the concept when I had time.

At home that evening, I spotted the action item amongst my many notes from the day. I was curious and wanted to know more, so I did some online searches. I didn't find much. This was a brand-new concept and there was very little information about how blogs worked or what they were being used for. Eventually, after some digging, I found some weblogs, including a couple created by people I knew at Microsoft. The creators even had a fancy word for themselves: bloggers. Most of the content of these weblogs was too technical for me; there was stuff about writing code, data encryption, and bug squashing. But I remember enjoying one short post about how to fix paper jams in a laser printer. That's what got me thinking about broader applications for blogs.

Weblogs seemed to offer potential far beyond their current use within the technical community. I started imagining the kinds of information I might share if I had my own weblog. A few searches later, I landed on a university website that offered anyone a free weblog. I signed up, gave my new blog a name, *The Useful Technology Blog*, and cautiously posted a few words to say hello to the world.

The next day, I wanted to share my news. 'Hey boss,' I said proudly, 'I'm a blogger!' He was intrigued, but not surprised! I explained what I had done, what I thought I might do with my weblog, and then anxiously asked if it was OK for me to do this as a Microsoft employee. To my relief, he said yes, and asked for a link to my blog so he could check it out himself. I had my first follower!

The next week, my manager announced to the team meeting 'Hey, I'm a blogger!' My curiosity had amplified his. Sadly, of the dozen or so people in that meeting where I first heard the word 'weblog', only my manager and I had the impulse to explore this new opportunity so deeply. The others ignored the idea with some only joining the party months or years later. Perhaps their instincts didn't draw them towards this new possibility, or maybe they didn't see it as their job to experiment or explore. It takes courage and ambition to be a pioneer, but it's rarely as challenging as some people make out.

I began sharing a post each morning to *The Useful Technology Blog*. It became a simple, enjoyable habit. On arriving at work, I would fire up my laptop, grab a cup of coffee, and allow myself up to thirty minutes to post the day's blog entry. My hour-long daily commute gave me ample time to think about what I might write, and by the time I took that first sip of office coffee, I was raring to go.

Here's what I did. My job, looking after marketing for Microsoft's email technologies, gave me the topic for many of my posts. I shared tips, tricks, workarounds, and a host of lesser-known features in the software. The greatest—and most unexpected—benefit of writing my daily blog was the joy of discovering and sharing something new every day. I didn't start out as an email expert but soon became one through hundreds of brief research and writing exercises. Comments and feedback posted by readers of my blog also gave me a boost and reminded me I was helping not just myself but people all over the world.

The simple act of sharing ideas forced me to structure my thoughts and be as factual and trustworthy as possible. But it also gave me a reason to form an opinion about topics that were relevant to my work. Taking a stance on whether something is good or bad helped to build my authority as a thought leader, which in turn made it easier to reach more people who might benefit from my expertise. Frankly, without expressing an opinion, I would not have had much to write about each day! Learning to take a side quickly became second nature and I was happy to share my thoughts about the pros and cons of Microsoft's latest innovations. This didn't mean I had to be controversial or provocative, but I had to learn to express my opinion in a concise, constructive way. For me, becoming a blogger proved to be a hugely helpful part of my learning journey.

How will you learn about your *thing?* There are so many ways to learn something new today, it pays to think about what may be best for you. There are common routes to learning like reading books or doing a training course, but also less obvious ways to learn like watching a TV documentary or interviewing experts online.

Use this page to list some interesting ways you could start your REACT journey of learning about your *thing.*

CHAPTER 10

OPEN - YOUR CURIOSITY SUPERPOWER

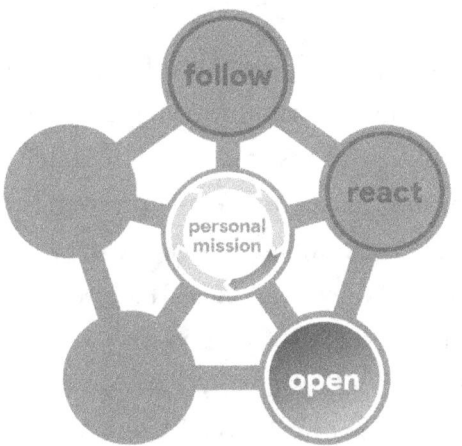

OPEN is the first of three human superpowers in the
ReadyAlready Growth Cycle that you will unleash on
your *thing* to uncover fresh possibilities and opportunities
for your future. It's all about using your natural curiosity
to question the way things are and identify areas where
improvements may be possible.

But first, why do I call OPEN a human superpower?
Artificial intelligence (AI) systems and automated

computing tools are remarkably good at answering questions and finding solutions to problems, but they are truly lousy at doing this with the kind of biological human thinking that your brain excels at. To be truly curious, you need to suspend your past experience and pose naïve, sometimes almost childlike, questions that others might be afraid to ask. Computers cannot do this as well as you can because they make sense of language and problems by replicating patterns in existing data sets. They cannot be humanly curious, but you can.

Without data, a computer is nothing. The human brain, however, is capable of thinking independently and filtering its thoughts through consciousness to see fresh possibilities. This biological thinking process is profoundly different to the linear way that computers organise data, and is unlikely to ever be bettered by machines. That's why OPEN is such a vital skill to develop as it gives you an edge over all future automated tools and systems. When you know how to use your human superpowers, you'll become indispensable at work for as long as you wish to be there. No AI system will ever be able to take your job!

The OPEN step then, is all about curiosity, the human superpower that will help you understand your current world more deeply, before you explore possible future solutions in the following step. OPEN allows you to suspend your experience and expertise before asking questions with a beginner's mind about your *thing*. It's about allowing your mind to explore new realities by putting your experience and knowledge and wisdom to one side, and asking brilliant questions that challenge the status quo. Let's look at how OPEN can free up your mind to see opportunities for improvement.

If you watched a home video about your life ten years ago, you might cringe. 'Oh my goodness, what was I doing with my hair?!' 'Why was I talking like that?' 'What was that outdated camera I was using?' Everything looks archaic when we cast our minds back a few years, and the same is true for the present day. At this moment, everything feels current, but it's all going to change. Right now, everything feels up-to-date and modern, but it won't stay that way for long. Your experience is rooted in the past and the present, both of which lose their relevance with each passing day. As you'll see, OPEN invites you to temporarily suspend your current reality so you can start to see new possibilities for the next.

If you want to create a brighter future as you chase down your Personal Mission, you have to be curious in the present so you can spot opportunities for improvement that could re-shape your tomorrow. It's that sort of muscle you need to build. In REACT, you locked on to the *thing* you really like, and now it's time to explore it from lots of different angles. To do this fully, you need to ditch any and all preconceptions about it. You'll need to abandon all assumptions about your *thing* and park any prior expectations of what it could or couldn't become. For example, perhaps your *thing* is getting really good at negotiation in the future. If that's your *thing*, and you've seen people negotiate, and maybe even done it yourself, you'll know if someone is good or bad at it. But, here's the difficult part: You need to *abandon* that awareness. Let go of that previous knowledge. You need to trick your brain into acting as though it is discovering the art and science of negotiation for the very first time.

With OPEN, you are trying to shift from seeing what you *want* to see to what you *need* to see. In this step, you're actively eliminating the unhelpful pull of confirmation bias, where you may only pay attention to possibilities that confirm what you already believe. You need to look at your *thing* differently and explore the whole truth and all of its magical possibilities.

In my talks, I sometimes reference a Zen Buddhism concept called Shoshin. This translates roughly to 'beginner's mind'. Buddhists are required to read the same prayer texts again and again throughout their whole lives. When they read each day, they are taught not to bring in any preconceptions, just to read the text afresh and to see what the prayer says to them in that moment. The practice of Shoshin, bringing a beginner's mind to a task, helps Buddhists gain new understanding and enlightenment each day. I like this concept because it shows that when you suspend your prejudgments and use a beginner's mind, like Shoshin, you can start seeing fresh possibilities for what something can mean, can be, and can become. This is what we're trying to do with OPEN. Imagine how much more perceptive, alert, and alive you could be if you could approach each working day with an open, beginner's mind.

The way to do this is easy to describe but tricky to do: Suspend your experience. If you're thinking about something at work, trick your brain by imagining it's your first day there, ever. You've just walked through the door, and everything is new to you. You don't know where your desk is or how to use the elevator. Now, if it were your first day at work, what would you do differently? What would you pay attention to? What would you notice that perhaps you've long since stopped paying attention to? And what questions might you ask to help you make sense of your new surroundings and responsibilities?

The best curiosity questions often start with 'Why?' If you've ever spent time with young children, you'll know they ask 'Why?' a lot. In fact, they ask 'Why?' nearly all the time. 'Why are we going to the shops?' 'Why do we need groceries?' 'Why are we walking there?' 'Why must I put on my shoes?' 'Why do I need a coat?' Young children ask these incessant 'Why?' questions to help them make sense of new things and feel safe in their world. Adults tend not to ask 'Why?' as much, but we can learn a lot from rediscovering some of our lost childlike curiosity. An audience member once told me that her university professor had taught her that 'WHY' stands for 'Will Help You'. I love that idea, and she was right. A well-timed 'Why?' can help you unlock all kinds of fresh possibilities for the future. It really 'will help you.'

As an experienced worker, if you're facing an issue at work, you might say, 'We should do this', because your experience has taught you the value of finding a solution. 'We should order more stock', or 'We should have a sale in January'. But when you use a truly open, curious mind, you are more likely to ask yourself, 'Why do we have stock?', or 'Why do we have a sale?', or 'Why do it in January?' The answer to these naïve questions may well turn out to be obvious, but if you've never asked them before, you might be surprised how often they reveal potential areas for improvement or positive changes. With each 'Why?' you'll be consciously questioning the way things are, not because you assume these aspects are suboptimal, but because you want to make sense of them and detect where changes might be beneficial. And then, instead of robotically ordering more stock or slashing your prices in January, you could start to explore some new possibilities. As you'll see in the next step, SURPRISE, instead of instinctively saying 'We should...' you may find yourself saying 'We could...' Now that's an exciting place for reinvention to begin!

But let's get back to OPEN and consider why it's such an important skill for thriving in our fast-changing world. Marshall McLuhan, the Canadian philosopher, had this phrase we used to love at Microsoft, 'Today if something works, it's obsolete.' Bill Gates, for a period of time, shared that message in meetings to wake colleagues up to how quickly the world was changing, and how much innovation was now possible. This mindset helped us accept that our products were never finished and we would always be playing catch-up to innovations that were being created each day by clever people around the world. When you accept that philosophy—that practically everything you know can already be done faster, cheaper, better—you give yourself absolute permission to question everything and to intelligently decide if and how it could be improved. And when you're comfortable questioning everything, you will start to see opportunities for improvements everywhere!

A warning at this stage: Having an open mind may make you feel a little vulnerable. Quietly pondering seemingly daft questions may feel uncomfortable, even a little embarrassing, at first. This does take humility and bravery to go through. But think of this: If your laptop caught on fire, you wouldn't be embarrassed to ask, 'Where's the fire extinguisher?' You'd have no hesitation, and probably yell the question at the top of your voice. You'd get on it, quickly assessing the situation and finding a solution. It's OK to ask that question. It is really OK to ask a lot of questions. Not asking would be far worse for everyone.

Just because something seems right today doesn't make it right tomorrow. And with a little investigation and curiosity, you may discover many things about your work that don't even make sense today. Some working practices may have made sense once, but over the passage of time they've become part of a routine, an established process, just 'the way things get done around here'. If no-one ever questions why we're doing certain things, we may never spot how out-of-date our ways of working have become. You can be that questioner and be fascinated by your work and your *thing* anew. It's surprisingly easy finding aspects of your work that could be improved when you start with an open mind and the knowledge that everything is already obsolete and ripe for improvement.

To excel at OPEN, ask yourself: Why? Think about your *thing,* the work you do, and your Personal Mission. You have to look at your world with fresh eyes and ask, 'Why is X like that?' If it were your first day at work, you might wonder, 'Why is the copier in the corridor?' and the answer might come back from a colleague that it's always been there. But if you explore the topic further by asking 'Why has it always been there?' you might discover that the corridor is where the installation guy first plugged the machine in, long before the office was last rearranged. That original photocopier, long since replaced with a smaller, quieter model, might now fit perfectly in the empty corner of the office, which would be more convenient for everyone. That's an example of a workplace 'Why?' Or: 'Why does the company coffee shop close at 3pm, when most people work until 5pm? Maybe they have a good reason, or maybe no-one ever asked the question before. If you're curious about your *thing,* you must ask that question!

These sorts of 'Why?' questions may sound inane. Yet, those are often the best ones to start with. 'Why is the Monday meeting always on a Monday?' If you don't know, you have to ask that, even though the answer already seems to be hidden in the question!. Perhaps a former boss once had a Monday meeting, and then it just stuck, leaving everyone in a perpetual cycle of starting every week in a dreary meeting. If you're thinking about negotiation skills, ask the obvious questions like 'Why do people negotiate?' You may think you don't need to ask that question, but you do. 'Why does losing a negotiation feel bad?' 'Why do negotiations take time?' 'Why is a win-win outcome desirable?' 'Why do some negotiations fail?' 'Why is it even called negotiation?' Brilliant, childlike questions like these may help prise open your mind to an avalanche of new possibilities for the future.

Very importantly, at this point, we're not trying to find solutions. We're just trying to awaken our curiosity for the topic and ask questions that may lead us to a better understanding. So, for example, asking 'Why is a win-win outcome desirable?' is a valid, curiosity-fuelled question, but asking 'Why don't we aim to win sixty per cent of negotiations?' is pre-loaded with a possible solution. Great OPEN questions are expansive; they create room for more possibilities, they don't zero in on just one solution. That's why they usually start with 'Why…?', not 'Why don't we…?'

I use OPEN to help me make sense of situations all the time. Back in my days at Kimberly-Clark, I would often ask, 'Why?' 'Why are we having this meeting?' 'Why are shoppers happy to spend more on groceries at Christmas?' 'Why are there no instructions for use on our bathroom tissue packaging?' These were the simple, naïve, sometimes fun questions few would dare ask, but I often uncovered profound truths in the answers. Many times, I would first ask these questions of myself, not out loud in meetings. And if a reasonable answer didn't come to me quickly, I'd pluck up the courage to speak up. To ease my embarrassment at asking a seemingly silly 'Why?' question, I'd often say, 'Sorry, I'm "new" here', even though I'd been at the company for years. 'New' was always tongue-in-cheek.

There's even some truth to my playfulness. We're all new when we start out at work, but if the context in which you're working is changing all the time, every day is an opportunity to look at it afresh. If you don't approach work this way, you may soon find yourself becoming set in your ways, thinking conventional thoughts, accepting the perceived wisdom of the organisation, and tolerating aspects of your work that could easily be improved. You'll eventually become conservative, unambitious, and invested in protecting the status quo rather than a progressive, driven, forward thinker who is keen to unearth new possibilities.

Here are the steps to beginning the OPEN process:

Step 1: Build your 'Why?' Muscle. In some of my talks, I'll say, 'Who has a "why" question about this meeting room?' Audience members are often embarrassed to volunteer a suggestion at first, worried they will look silly in front of their peers. To develop your curiosity, I recommend you first do this in the safety of your own home. Ask yourself a 'why' question about anything you can observe. 'Why are there curtains in this room?', 'Why are they made of fabric?', 'Why do they come in pairs?', 'Why do they hang from the top of the window?' 'Why is the curtain rail straight?' With a few seemingly naïve 'why' questions, you will quickly become more acutely aware of your surroundings and maybe even spot some things that could be improved. Remember: You're not trying to find solutions just yet. You may instinctively jump to conclusions, like imagining replacing the curtains with blinds or shutters. But your primary goal in OPEN is to use your brilliant human curiosity to become more aware of how things are, so you get a feel for where future improvements might be possible. Try to delay your natural inclination to identify what those improvements could be, but do be prepared to gently challenge some established conventions, and maybe question some experience-driven behaviours.

Step 2: Inject some variety and novelty into your life with new, simple rituals. To help you build your curiosity muscle even further, break some well-worn habits and try something new. For example, you could grab your morning coffee from a different shop—or even get a Matcha instead of your usual Tall, Non-Fat, Caramel Macchiato with an extra shot. Stir up your commute by taking a different route or mode of transport to work. Read a new magazine, newspaper, or journal. By introducing new experiences into life in small, regular doses, you'll be exploring life's options and injecting space for even more curiosity in your daily routine. You have to build that muscle; it won't build itself.

Have some fun with this and be prepared to look at any part of your life afresh. Why do you do things a certain way? Why do you like X, but dislike Y? Why, why, why…? The more you ask why, the bigger and more powerful your curiosity muscles will grow, and the more open your mind will be to dreaming up bold, new possibilities in the next step in the ReadyAlready Growth Cycle.

Step 3: Consider 'quick wins'. What small steps could lead to big changes in your life? If certain things are easy to implement, why not just do them today? If, for example, you asked yourself, 'Why do I carry a laptop to work every day?', 'Why do I get nervous before a meeting with my boss?', 'Why do I feel so tired around mid-afternoon?' Simple questions like these can unlock easy, quick-win solutions that may have been staring you in the face for years. Simply making the space to consider the 'Why?' can open up easy opportunities for improvements in many parts of your life.

While it's important to ask these seemingly obvious questions, it's also worth checking that they relate to your Personal Mission in some way. This will help you to keep in mind what you're trying to achieve in the long run. Remind yourself of your Personal Mission and who you are most hoping to help through your work. You don't want to lose sight of the bigger opportunity. It's all about what you're doing in the service of others, the long-term difference you're making to their lives. Your Personal Mission keeps your eyes on the prize so you're not being pulled in a bunch of different directions. It helps you move forward, using child-like, open-minded curiosity combined with baby steps in a structured way.

Once you've mastered the skill of OPEN, it will become a joyful and uplifting habit for a lifetime. It's liberating to have the courage to question things, knowing that not everything is buttoned up. Some things are just completely nuts and will stay that way until someone like you has the wisdom to question and explore them more deeply. With OPEN, you not only become more insightful, but you start to see the things that your experience misled you into believing were that way for a good reason. Once again, this is a process of exercising your humility and honesty. There are also many things that you don't yet know about your work and OPEN is a super simple way to bring them into focus and understand them more fully. An open mind gives you an eagerness to explore along with the energy you need to discover afresh. Done well, it's a really joyous part of the process. So, have fun with it and stay curious.

Reader Recap: OPEN.

On gaining experience. With so much change coming at us, it's much easier to *gain* experience than it is to *stay* experienced. But to gain experience, you need to be open to seeing things differently, not simply accepting conventional wisdom or believing everything that your colleagues tell you. You need to make your own discoveries, to form your own opinions, not robotically trot out the same lines as everyone else.

- **On habits, and being ready to break some.** We need habits to be efficient and get through each working week intact. But some become so ingrained we don't even know they're there: scanning our phone for messages with bleary eyes first thing in the morning, commuting the same boring route each day, unthinkingly treating yourself to an expensive cappuccino and croissant before you start work. Many habits are helpful and harmless, but others can inadvertently become sources of stress in our lives (like always reaching for an alcoholic drink at the end of a busy day, complaining about work to family and friends, or checking emails from colleagues late into the evening). To create space for personal growth, you may need to suspend some bad habits, rituals, and mindsets, and shift them into something more positive and helpful for your future. That might mean reading a novel instead of those emails from your boss or going for a walk with a friend rather than drowning your sorrows in Cabernet Sauvignon.

- **On curiosity.** If you've not been actively curious in a while, you may need to take dramatic action. Next time you do anything, try to do it in a way that is different to your established conventions. If you are thirsty, choose a beverage you've never had before or that you would usually avoid. If you're getting ready for work, use a completely different decision process to select what to wear. If you're going to a meeting, choose a different seat at the table or sit differently. Heck, you could even stay standing if you like! Approach every meeting like it's the first one you've ever been invited to. Some of your experiments will fail (I've yet to find a way to look good wearing red and yellow clothes), but others may be rejuvenating, refreshing, and deliciously intriguing. The goal is not to discover a better way to live your life immediately; it's to build your curiosity muscles little by little, day by day, making space for novelty and variety to creep into your life. In time, you might uncover some exciting opportunities for improvements in your life, many of which may already be close to home.

- **On developing a childlike curiosity about your** *thing.* We lose our childlike curiosity as we grow older. With experience, we have less interest or hunger for learning. We either accept that we don't need to know everything or we convince ourselves we know enough about most things to no longer be actively curious. Children don't have this limitation. They ask questions to make sense of the world and to feel safe within it. They have no qualms about being judged for the questions they ask, or fear of being demoted for asking a silly question. Children live in a perpetual state of wonder, discovering new things at every turn, and asking questions to explore how these things could be of use to them. If only adults could rediscover this skill and bring it back into the workplace. That's OPEN.

- Note: It takes courage to be and remain curious. Some of your questions, if voiced out loud, may seem like a threat to conventional thinking or the established order. You may upset the apple cart and be seen as a direct threat to leaders who have built their reputation on stacking those apples in a very precise way. But know that, in the long run, staying ahead of change demands that you sometimes act boldly. If you are not even prepared to ask questions about that apple cart, you run the risk of someone *else* stepping in and creating a new future on their terms instead of yours. Here's a quick formula to help keep this in your mind: OPEN = Active curiosity + purposeful questioning.

- **On how work beats the curiosity out of you.** The longer an organisation has been a player in its field, the less curious its employees are likely to be. Without intervention, even the most creative, innovative companies can lose their spark and get stuck in a rut of their own design. They stop asking naïve questions, leaning back on established conventions and norms, doing what they think is proven, right, or efficient. They obsess over answering questions, showing off their knowledge, proving that their elevated status and success are justified. Shifting from showing how much you know to exploring what you may need to know next will help. In a world of constant change, it pays to be a learn-it-all, not a know-it-all. Stay open-minded and curious; you'll thank me later!

Use this space to write some OPEN questions of your own. Thinking about your *thing*, what naïve questions could you ask about it and how it relates to your work? Remember, great OPEN questions are fuelled by curiosity and begin with 'Why...?'. They seek only to surface understanding, not to solve the problem itself by incorporating possible solutions.

Use the space below to jot down some 'Why...?' questions about your *thing*.

CHAPTER 11

SURPRISE - UNLEASHING PLAYFUL CREATIVITY ON YOUR *THING*

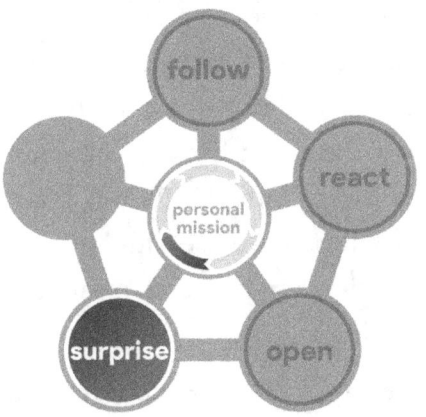

L et's get into our next superpower—SURPRISE! This is the step where you get to dream up potential applications for your *thing* with unexpected creativity and playfulness. It's a fun step, where you may even surprise yourself with some of the thoughts you have. By going through the first three steps, you were able to identify a useful *thing* to follow, validate that *thing* after conducting careful research and learning, and then challenge the status quo with childlike curiosity. And now you can really go wild!

Fun fact: When I first developed this model, I originally referred to the SURPRISE step as 'Wonder'. I chose this word because when you see your world with a sense of wonder, you are more likely to have big dreams about what you could do next with your life. Those moments when you're in a state of wonder, like when you visit a treasured historical building or amazing travel destination, allow you to connect with just how remarkable our world is. However, in the routine trudge through your hectic daily life, you've precious few opportunities to gaze in wonder. In fact, you may take many extraordinary things, like wi-fi, access to clean water, or the beauty of a sunrise, completely for granted. 'Wonder' seemed like a great word for this step, but in the end, I went with SURPRISE, to keep the FROST acronym going but also because without surprising yourself and others, making original and meaningful changes is almost impossible.

To embrace the SURPRISE step, you may first find it helpful to stop taking things for granted, and start being grateful that you are living through this time. When you value the miracle of the office printer, or being able to see your parcel delivery nearing your address on a map, or the calming nature of a hug, your brain can begin to engage with SURPRISE. By appreciating the majesty of our world, we make the idea of dreaming up new possibilities that might enhance our lives more accessible and enticing.

Then, and only then, can you appreciate the full wonder of your *thing* and do everything you can to harness its potential to improve the future.

During SURPRISE, you get to dream, fantasise, and finesse some potentially wild ideas that may help transport your *thing* to another level. SURPRISE is your time for creativity and play.

When explaining this step to business teams, I often see worried and anxious looks around the room. Creativity is a scary word for many people, but I want you to push through any nervousness and try. Whether you're an actuary or a zoologist, you are still a vital, artistic person—even if you're not technically an 'artist'. The rule with creativity is that you are only as creative as you believe you can be. Trust me, you're just as capable of having interesting ideas as anyone else. As you work in this step, my goal for you is that you turn some aspects of your day job into a daydream, and find the courage and headspace to imagine new possibilities. I want you to feel ready to welcome the coming surprises into your life, knowing that they relate to your *thing* and may prove valuable to your future. Just be prepared to work on this, and you may soon find yourself getting addicted (in the best way) to the insanely pleasurable feeling of not knowing exactly where you're going, but at the same time being excited to be on the journey.

That's what SURPRISE is all about.

Before we get into our exercise, I want you to banish all creativity-stunting phrases from your mind. This is a bit like what you did during OPEN: You need to prevent yourself from saying, 'Oh, the boss won't like that suggestion', or 'That's not how we do stuff around here'. That closed, predetermined mindset will undoubtedly hold you back. A brilliant idea you may have to solve a problem that customers don't even know they have is still a brilliant idea. To avoid stunting your own creativity, I encourage you to have a questioning but playful mind that allows new ideas to enter your head, where you can toss them around a bit. Just try to have some ideas and have fun playing with them. The risk for you here is close to zero. The sky won't fall in if you don't have a new idea, but many people may benefit from a nice improvement if you try. So, the real risk here is not dreaming up some new concepts to explore in the first place. Just have a go!

Remember this as well: Your human creativity works in ways that are far better than AI, supercomputers, and any future technology we are likely to see. The reason for this is that creativity from your human brain benefits from the biological thinking process that allows you to consider loosely related but relevant stimuli in your pursuit of a novel idea. Computers are great at generating random ideas or using pre-existing information to offer a seemingly novel idea, but they cannot and never will be able to do this as well as your brilliant human brain.

Be prepared to make space for things to get a little surreal, too. Sometimes you have to trick your brain when you're having unexpected thoughts, otherwise it will follow the well-worn paths of what's 'expected' or 'been done before'. Don't take anything for granted. Instead, be aware of and grateful for each and every little discovery. This mindset will deepen your understanding of your *thing,* and help you see more imaginative ways to leverage it in your future work.

For a moment, consider everything whirling around you. It's quite amazing, actually. There's something transformational about appreciating the miracle of your work and the times we're living in. Think about how easy and low cost it is to have a video call with someone on the other side of the planet. Or the majesty of being able to flush a toilet and not worry about where that stuff goes. Seriously, our modern lives are hyper-convenienced and remarkable, yet we rarely stop to appreciate how fortunate we are. When you take the time to marvel at all that's around you and to appreciate how many things have improved during your lifetime, you'll value everything more highly. Become more sensitive to the improvements and new opportunities that are opening up in your life. Then you'll be excited to help create an even richer life for yourself and others. For me, I still love to surprise myself and my colleagues with a unique thought, not because I want to impress others, but because to give birth to a great idea and gift it to others is a remarkable privilege. Nearly everything you know and have started out as an idea in someone's head. Where might your ideas take you?

The people who are changing the world lean into the SURPRISE process naturally. They never stop. They constantly think about what's possible and how they can improve their reality. While you go through this chapter, allow new ideas to come to the surface. Much like the OPEN step we covered in the previous chapter, this requires some childlike skills, suspending fears of being judged or critiqued and simply having ideas for the fun of it. They're all within you; over time, you've just learned how to suppress them in a grown-up, businesslike environment that doesn't always value or reward novel thought. But no good change ever happened without someone having the initial idea!

Get your paper and pen ready, and let's go SURPRISE ourselves.

Step 1: Take a moment to think about when you have the best ideas.

There are certain points in your days when you're naturally more creative. My audiences tell me they have lots of their best thoughts in the bath, walking the dog, in the shower, or with their morning coffee. I've learned, over the years, that my most creative moment each day is when I'm just exiting sleep and waking up—when I'm half asleep and my brain is starting to think about the day ahead. Many of the ideas in my talks have been dreamt up during that weird in-between space. To capture that moment, I keep a notepad by my bed. When I find myself in that in-between state, I enjoy the swirling, meandering way my brain is thinking and leave it alone to do its magic. It's a fine line to walk, and I get better at it each time. Most importantly, I try to capture my ideas by scribbling them into my notebook as soon as I am ready to get up. I'd forget too quickly otherwise!

Perhaps the in-between time is when you get your best ideas too, or maybe it happens in an environment that's unique to you. Maybe it's during exercise, when you're buzzing with endorphins. Maybe it's when you're relaxing at home, maybe while preparing dinner, and not distracted by the pressures of work. Think about when you tend to have the most ideas and consider what's making that possible. Is it the lack of distractions, the place, your energy level, the time of day? Identify what makes your imagination work best and prepare for and sanctify that environment. And always keep a pen and paper nearby, or the notes app on your phone, so you can capture any fresh ideas before they leave you!

What I've learned in working with hundreds of organisations is that you can't easily do the SURPRISE step in a workshop or busy team environment. You can't just turn this stuff on! That's why those horrible brainstorming sessions at work generate such mediocre ideas. Being creative only happens when you are in the right biological and physiological state. And when you understand your unique preferences and style, you can optimise your creative output by recreating the environment that works for you. Once you are in the right place, you can really start asking questions and surprising yourself by wondering, 'What if we do this?' 'What if we try that?' 'What if we use data from customer service to do x, y, and z?' With practice, your starter questions will get more and more specific, and instinctively more closely aligned with your *thing* and your Personal Mission.

Step 2: Once you're in your zone of SURPRISE, begin searching for and unearthing those new ideas associated with your *thing*.

This is where you get really expansive in your thinking. You want to explode your *thing* with an injection of unexpected creativity. And there's a really simple way to spark new ideas: Just ask 'What if...' So, rather than thinking 'We could' or 'How about...', simply begin your idea with 'What if...' and then finish the sentence with whatever comes to mind. That's it. You don't need to answer the 'What if...' question, and you don't have to cross-examine the idea and identify everything that's wrong about it. You're just trying to stumble upon the germ of some ideas. No judgement, just possibilities to explore. This is the start of the ideation process, not the end.

Don't worry if what you dream up might be outlandish, wacky, or unexpected for your colleagues, your competitors, and even you. Let the ideas come to you by simply jotting down thoughts about how you could address some of the challenges and opportunities you uncovered for your *thing* during REACT and OPEN. The key thing here is getting down lots of ideas. It doesn't matter if they're far-fetched or unreasonable. For once, it's OK to go for quantity, not quality! Have fun with this process. If you're enjoying the journey, your mind will reward you with another idea. Smile to yourself, have an idea, write it down, and repeat.

Here's an example of how this might work. If your *thing* was getting better at time management, the SURPRISE stage may allow you to dream up some quite unexpected solutions. During REACT you may have learned about some great techniques for time management and realised how common an issue this is for busy professionals. Then in OPEN you will have questioned 'Why?' Some of your naïve questions might have been 'Why am I often late to meetings?' 'Why do I take so little time for lunch?' 'Why are deadlines often short?' and 'Why do I always have to catch up on work emails on Sundays?' These simple questions will have opened up space in your mind for new possibilities, but they won't have delivered any possible solutions. That's where the SURPRISE step comes in.

Now, using creative thinking, you can begin dreaming up some 'What if...?' questions to help you surface novel possibilities to improve time management for you and your work colleagues. 'What if I wore a watch on both wrists so I'm more aware of the time?' or 'What if I blocked out fifteen minutes before each meeting to prepare?' or 'What if I rewarded colleagues with cake for being on time?' These nascent ideas may not be earth-shattering or life-changing or even feasible, but if you keep going, imagining lots and lots of possibilities, before long you may have some genuinely intriguing and potentially viable solutions on your hands. 'What if my company became world-famous for always being on time?' 'What if we gave our suppliers free training called 'The Secrets of Never Being Late?' 'What if our IT team blocked the email app on Sundays?...'

Someone clever once told me that much of being creative is little more than the process of smashing together two previously disconnected things. That's an oversimplification of a complex cognitive process, but it's a great place to start. So, if your time management is lousy, you could take the idea of being late and combine it with something random like a bottle of water. Your colleagues might not thank you for spraying them with water when they arrive late to your meeting, but at least you've had an idea! If you're feeling creatively stuck, try combining two more previously unrelated things and see what your mind can dream up. Just keep going. Give it a try, it's fun!

While you do this, keep your Personal Mission in mind. Remember why you're working through the ReadyAlready Growth Cycle: to make something about the world better in the service of others. But don't let that notion constrain you or stifle your creativity. Use it as fuel to keep going, the energy you need, because you really want to improve the world in some way. Your Personal Mission alone may not give you the answers, but it will give you the motivation to stay focused, keep trying, and maybe land on some ideas that seem to have potential. Again, just keep going. Creativity sometimes takes time. More ideas will come if you work at it.

In addition, having a clearly defined problem to solve in your mind may help. Think about what your *thing* is, and the sort of area you want to apply it to in your work. Again, if the *thing* you chose in the FOLLOW step was improving your personal time management, one of the problems you might wish to solve could be helped by stating the problem as a question like: 'How can I feel more alive in the evenings (and less like an exhausted work zombie!)?' That's a silly example, I know, but sometimes a fun problem can spark better creativity and more interesting ideas. When the problem you need to solve is well defined, it's a little like going bowling with the gutter guards up. As long as you stay focused on the task, eventually you'll knock over some pins!

Step 3: When it's not flowing, take a break.

Don't stress if the ideas don't pour out of you the first time you try. Just keep bouncing ideas and potential solutions around in your mind and keep your pen and paper to hand. You may even want to stop, take a break, and go for a walk to see what your brain comes up with when it's not laser-focused on your *thing*. Crucially, don't judge your ideas. Greenhouse them. Think of them like little seedlings that are incredibly fragile. If you meddle with them too much or stomp all over them, they're going to die. Instead, look after your ideas, give them some time to grow and develop in your imagination, and allow them to become stronger in their own time. Sleep on your ideas. Let them rest in the greenhouse of your mind, and revisit them to keep them watered and to see which grow into a beautiful flower of opportunity!

Step 4: Even if you look at all your ideas and find nothing there, they may still be valuable.

With consistent practice and time spent in a relaxed but actively creative state (like for me, right before I get up each morning), you may realise something about your ideas that you didn't notice on the first pass. Just stick with this practice and you will see encouraging results. Come back to your ideal idea-generating state with curiosity and your Personal Mission in mind, and those 'nothing' ideas may eventually develop into 'something' you can actually share with others. We'll discuss the sharing process in the TELL step. And, best of all, even if your ideas are half-baked, you will have something to work with, something to refine and improve with help from others. As long as you have something, you've aced the SURPRISE stage.

In summary, SURPRISE is your permission to have ideas, bold dreams, and to start dreaming up new possibilities that may have a positive impact on your future. Sure, you may have a boatload of bad ideas, but you only need one good seedling of an idea to potentially transform your world. It's a vital step in the process, maybe the genesis of a future-enhancing, potentially life-changing idea. By following this framework, you are effectively laying the foundations for your future by becoming the person who first unearths new possibilities. You may even discover a novel idea you can make happen and introduce to the world. You're transforming the careful choice you made in FOLLOW, you're using what you learned and decided in REACT, you're making use of what curiosity showed you in OPEN, and now moulding all that stuff into some unexpected, non-obvious, but potentially valuable ideas for the future.

SURPRISE will give you a bunch of initial ideas for your *thing* that may be wacky, half-baked, and completely fanciful. And that's OK! With the fifth and final step, TELL, you'll see how collaborating with your colleagues can give your ideas wings and even help some of them take flight.

Reader Recap: SURPRISE.

- **On getting started with SURPRISE:** Get addicted to that pleasurable feeling of not knowing but being on a journey to finding out. Welcome surprises into your life. Banish creativity-stunting phrases like 'That's *not* how we do it', 'We've tried that already', or 'I already know what customers want'. Have a go! You're not launching a space mission, you're trying to make your future working life more interesting by exploring new ways to achieve your Personal Mission. Unless you come up with something truly dangerous and daft, nothing bad will happen if you simply have a few fresh ideas!

- **On the struggle of not feeling creative at work:** Don't start by trying to solve a major project or by radically re-engineering large parts of the business. Start small. Inject some creativity into your work life with a simple task like rearranging the mugs in the staff kitchen or pinning some family holiday photos on your desk. You'll quickly realise that creative expression is not threatening or risky, it's natural and fun!

- **On rediscovering a sense of wonder in what is possible:** You'll remember that I originally named the SURPRISE step as Wonder. People who exist in a positive state of wonder, who have an open-mouthed appreciation of just how incredibly remarkable our world is are often better at having creative thoughts because they are tuned into the miracle of our lives. Stop taking things for granted, start being grateful that you are living through this time, and all the wonders it contains.

- **On the importance of going bold with your ideas first:** Have fun, experiment with ideas, delve into thoughts your competitors won't dare to have. Don't worry if your ideas seem far-fetched or crazy; you can always rein them back in later. Keep going until you have some non-obvious thoughts that might just prove valuable in the future. But dream big first: You'll never have a breakthrough idea if you restrict yourself to thinking small.

Use this page to start dreaming of some novel ways that your *thing* might help you pursue your Personal Mission in the near-future. Be creative and have fun with this, being prepared to entertain even outlandish or patently ridiculous ideas. This is about quantity, not quality. Buried within lots of ideas you may just find the perfect idea for your future. Remember, SURPRISE questions usually begin with 'What if...', followed by a non-obvious, but hopefully valuable new idea.

Use your SURPRISE superpower to jot down lots of imaginative 'What if...' questions about your *thing*.

CHAPTER 12

TELL - SHARING TO WIN SUPPORT AND CREATE THE FUTURE

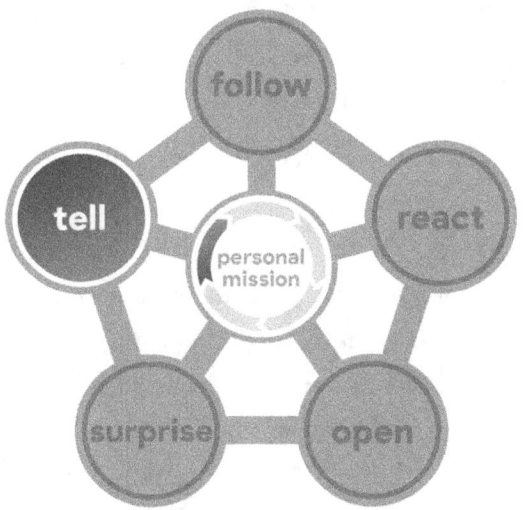

We're finally at the last step in your journey around the ReadyAlready Growth Cycle: TELL.

This is the third superpower that you can never delegate to technology, AI, or anything else that isn't a living, breathing, magical human being like you! It's an innate human skill that's going to help you create the future with the encouragement and support of others.

TELL is where you courageously share what you've been thinking about and some of the ideas you've had with a few of your work colleagues. The goal here is to win their interest and support so they can help you transform some of your nascent ideas into full-fledged realities. This is the transition point from thinking to doing. So far, this process has been largely a one-person mission. You may have chatted about what you're doing with a friendly colleague or partner along the way, but you've been doing most of the heavy lifting alone. Now, it's time to put a certain often-used proverb to good use: 'If you want to go fast, go alone. If you want to go far, go together.'

How often have you had an idea and not bothered to share it with someone else because you didn't think they'd be interested, or you were simply too embarrassed? An idea that stays trapped in the vacuum of your mind will never take off. It has to be out there, in the world, in other people's minds as well as your own. When you share it with the right people, you can accelerate along the road towards positive collective action that may bring meaningful improvements to the world. Plus, I can honestly say that I've never had an idea that wasn't improved in some way by sharing it with others. They either helped me improve the idea with their unique perspective or gave me the encouragement I needed to start believing I might be on the right track.

This step is so exciting because it's where you fundamentally kick-start the future. Something you've learned about, thought about, or dreamed about may just catch fire and become a force for positive change that improves the future for you and your colleagues. This part of the process is absolutely vital. It will give your ideas legs, helping you and others unleash the full potential of these concepts. Your goal is to share your hopes for the future and some of the early-stage ideas that you developed in the previous steps.

A word of caution: Before you proceed, I want you to know that this step, like some you have already worked through, requires you to be brave. It takes courage to have ideas, but even more to share them with work colleagues, so I'm going to give you a process that will make doing this easy. Just another reason why it's important to do these steps in order.

Remember: You cannot create meaningful, sustainable change alone. You need people to hear you, to make your ideas better, and maybe even turn them into reality. You've put in the preparation work, but unless you're a Leonardo da Vinci-style genius, your ideas are unlikely to be fully formed masterpieces. Tapping into the minds and energy of the right people will help you finesse them into something that will make others say, 'that's interesting, we should try that'. There are so many great ideas that have remained just that: a vague notion rattling about in someone's head because it hasn't been shared or allowed to grow with help from others. Or a cracking idea that's hurriedly mumbled out in the dying minutes of a team meeting when others just want to get back to their desks. Don't make those common mistakes: The way you TELL is as important as the topic and ideas you have to share. As Marshall McLuhan wrote, 'the medium is the message'. What this means is that *how* you communicate has a huge impact on the message that people will hear. Don't let your ideas get lost in the noise of busy work days—put them on a plinth so the right people can admire them! Every second you spend thinking about TELL will improve the end results you ultimately achieve from the overall process.

The question that immediately comes up when we think about this part of the ReadyAlready Growth Cycle is: Who should you TELL? This is so important. Consider the people you know at work, and perhaps outside, who will give you their time, listen willingly, and show interest in your work. Ultimately, you're hoping they may help you refine and improve your thinking, and maybe even join you in transforming the rough ideas into working concepts and tangible improvements for the organisation. If you TELL the 'wrong' people, they may suck the life out of your ideas by imposing too many of their own limiting beliefs on you, deflating your confidence and passion for the subject in the process. I've lost track of the number of times I made that rookie mistake early in my career. And don't just TELL your closest friends and family members; they'll likely be too polite or disinterested to give you truthful, helpful feedback.

Alternatively, if you tell too many people—perhaps making an announcement at the big company meeting— they may not feel personally invested enough to support you. And, conversely, if you tell too few people, you risk losing momentum. You need the right people, in the right place, at the right time. Good, helpful, generous people who are happy to listen to new ideas and support you by trying to make them even better.

Also, don't feel like you have to go straight to the big bosses with your ideas. In my talks, I explain why new, innovative, future-facing ideas rarely benefit from being exposed early on to what I call the HIPPO, the 'Highest Paid Person's Opinion'. This is likely the view of your boss or the big boss at work, the people who earn the big bucks and have the highest status in your workplace. The HIPPO's opinion carries weight because of their relative seniority and experience, but it is unlikely to be any more valuable to you at this stage than the opinions of your peers and colleagues. Predicting what will be successful in the future is notoriously difficult, mostly because the future hasn't happened yet! And the HIPPO in your workplace is unlikely to be any better at guessing than anyone else. Ultimately, their opinion will matter a lot because they may get to decide what happens and what doesn't, but right now, as you're bouncing your ideas around, HIPPOs can be hugely unhelpful and destructive. They may have authority and power, but they are no better at predicting the future than anyone else.

So, don't feel you have to go to the HIPPO to get permission just yet. That can wait. And if you are a HIPPO, good news: you're off the hook! You don't have to be the ultimate judge and jury for whether an idea for the future is good or bad. Instead, create a supportive environment and encourage your team to work together to make ideas better, before collectively deciding which is most likely to succeed.

It's a bit like if you were a contestant on the show *Who Wants to Be a Millionaire?* If you had a difficult question about the future, using your 'phone a friend' lifeline is almost certainly a bad idea. Even if your friend is an eminent futurologist, they probably won't know the answer. Instead, if you use your 'ask the audience' lifeline, you'll almost certainly get a better steer on the correct answer. A diverse but willing population of people will help you land on the most plausible solution. When it comes to the future, tapping into the wisdom of crowds can be a powerful tool. Best of all, you don't need a huge crowd, just a few hand-picked people that you trust to listen and help.

Here's the best thing about the TELL step: If you've been keeping notes of your progress through the ReadyAlready Growth Cycle, all that work will make the TELL step really easy. You made a list and picked your *thing* in FOLLOW, you gained some interesting knowledge about your *thing* in REACT, you've asked some naïve, curiosity-driven questions during OPEN, and you've hopefully started to develop a few novel ideas in SURPRISE. Now all you have to do is package that up, ready to TELL your story to a few people who will be happy to listen.

Let's take a look at the steps in TELL and see how you can do it:

Step 1: Recognise the courage you're using in the TELL step.

It takes courage to share a nascent, undeveloped, or untested idea. You may worry about opening yourself up to ridicule or criticism. Some people may see your ideas as silly or inconsequential, or perhaps they may feel threatened by your ambition and energy. That's why you need to create a place where ideas, dreams, and random musings can be aired safely, without fear of ridicule or judgement. You want your ideas to be handled with care, like the tiny saplings they are, and these ideas need to be given the space, time, and light to grow into something beautiful. But you must TELL. An idea in your head is nothing; you must courageously release it to the right people and welcome their constructive feedback and encouragement. Remember, you'll never have the best ideas alone (unless you're a polymath genius, or maybe a wizard!)

Step 2: Give yourself a pat on the back before you TELL.

As you prepare to share your ideas, remember that you're not doing this for gratitude or congratulations from others. You're doing this for yourself and your Personal Mission. So, take a moment to give yourself some credit. Recognise the powerful journey you have been on, what you've learned, and how far you've come. This is a real accomplishment, so take a few moments to pause, reflect and celebrate your achievements. You're doing great!

Step 3: Prepare your TELL session.

Now, all you need to do is gather up your findings and decide which bits you want to share. Literally, just prepare enough so you can tell a short story about what you've been doing, during Follow, React, Open, and Surprise. Share your Personal Mission and the FROST journey you've been on and then practise telling that story.

Rehearse what you would like to say to help you focus on the most important bits and to give you confidence that you really know your stuff. I like to rehearse my talks outside while walking, because it's a great way to get some fresh air and exercise. I know that if I can practise what I want to say in a busy street or woodland forest, doing it in a meeting room will be a piece of cake! I call these a 'walk-and-talk' and it's become my favourite way to practise what I want to say in a meeting, event, or conference. While I'm walking, I talk to myself out loud, but I wear headphones (without music playing) so anyone who sees me will assume I'm on a phone call, not talking to myself like someone who's having a breakdown! And I get to practise my story, hear my key points in my head, and repeat the important bits as many times as I need until I feel I know what I'm talking about. I carry notes too—there are no prizes here for memorising everything!—and I jot down any new ideas I have while walking. You could try that too, but preparing for TELL is really about finding what works for you.

But do practise, as many times as you can. In reality, you'll probably have just a few minutes, maybe a quarter of an hour, to share your thoughts, just enough to tell your story and keep your audience's attention. If you notice you have too much information to share, focus on the most interesting, relevant things, cutting out anything that isn't well-aligned with your Personal Mission or a high priority for your future.

Now you have your message, think about how you can best deliver it. A 4pm meeting in a drab office sideroom might not be the best way to share your story! Remember: 'The medium is the message' and how you TELL matters as much as what you have to say. Think creatively about some of the many ways you could host your TELL session. If your *thing* is improving the company's negotiation skills, why not invite your colleagues to meet you at a town market where haggling over prices is commonplace? If time management is your *thing*, schedule your meeting to start at 11.07am under the big clock at the railway station! If you're trying to improve the future for customers, meet at their office or in one of their locations. Some of these suggestions may seem outlandish, but I guarantee you will get better results from your TELL session if you think creatively about how best to deliver it. Consider different locations, unusual times of the week, distinctive presentation formats (you don't have to use PowerPoint and a projector, in fact, please don't!). So many meetings and gatherings at work are rigidly predictable and dull; it doesn't take a lot of imagination or effort to create an experience for your colleagues that is refreshing, memorable, and inspiring.

Then, it's just a case of scheduling the session, inviting a handful of nice people, and being brave enough to turn up and share your story.

Step 4: Set some ground rules for your TELL session.

Neil Mullarkey of The Comedy Store Players in London first introduced me to improvisational comedy (improv) in the 1990s, and I still perform in live theatre comedy shows from time to time. The improv I do usually involves two or more people performing an entertaining theatrical scene spontaneously, inspired by suggestions from the audience. The idea of performing on stage, without even a script to follow, fills most people, including me, with dread, but there's a foundational starter phrase that every improv student learns on day one: 'Yes, and...' The idea is that if the other person in the scene says or does something, you must accept that offer and try to build on it. Starting any response with the phrase 'Yes, and...' helps force this behaviour by ensuring you accept what the other person has offered ('Yes') and then add something helpful to move the scene forward (', and...').

This simple phrase, 'Yes, and...', can be the foundation for more constructive conversations in your TELL session because it gently nudges the audience's reactions towards positively building on what the last person said, rather than shooting them down in flames with a 'No, because...' response. It makes each contribution additive instead of destructive. You don't want the defeatist negativity of 'No, because...' in your TELL session, so ask your audience to try 'Yes, and...' instead.

To help instill this positivity into your TELL session, you could write those words on the flipchart or whiteboard, hand out 'Yes, and...' cards, or even wear a t-shirt emblazoned with the phrase! Just do whatever you must to encourage your TELL colleagues to be positive, additive, and constructively helpful. In her excellent book *Improv Your Life: An Improviser's Guide to Embracing Whatever Life Throws at You*, Pippa Evans describes how saying yes allows us to be more open to creative ideas and adventures. At the same time, 'Yes, and...' gives us a chance to be better shaped by the circumstances around us. That way, even when we are feeling vulnerable, we know that there will always be a next step to take, despite not knowing what that step will be—and that part, Pippa says, is thrilling! Give it a try!

Step 5: Remind yourself of your Personal Mission.
Just before your TELL session, you may find it helpful to reflect on your Personal Mission and remind yourself of the people who may be the most positively impacted by your ideas. Think about your customers, business partners, or colleagues, and how they may benefit if all goes well. Before I give a talk, I gently remind myself why I am there, how much I love my audience, and how much I want to help them become future-ready for life. I find this puts me into their service, so I deliver a talk that's inspired by them and tailored to their needs. By reconnecting with your Personal

Mission, you'll draw energy and passion from knowing you are doing something important that may improve the lives of the people you serve.

Step 6: Have the TELL session!

During the session, you'll put all of these steps into motion with your invited co-workers and trusted colleagues (no HIPPOs allowed!). I find that a nice audience size is three to five people. Any more and things may get too hectic; any fewer and you may not get the energetic, positive response you need. At the start, set some simple ground rules (e.g. 'Yes, and...'), and then share your Personal Mission and the story of your journey through FROST—FOLLOW, REACT, OPEN, SURPRISE, and now TELL. You'll quickly see which ideas light up your audience the most as they zero in on the suggestions that they feel have the most potential.

Here are a few additional rules you might like to share at the start of your session:

- Leave any hidden agendas at the door—everyone in the room is there to support the others

- Surrender any feelings of competition, we're in it to win it together

- Try to listen first until you see the big picture; we'll discuss everything later

- Evaluate any ideas based on the value they may bring to the people we serve (usually our customers or partners)

- If invited, the HIPPO (Highest Paid Person's Opinion) has the same weight here as everyone else
- Please join in with enthusiasm and bring some 'Yes, and...' positivity!

Step 7: Decide if your TELL session was successful.

The goal of your TELL session is to share what you've been working on, so you can hear constructive feedback and suggestions from others. You're aiming to find out which of your ideas, if any, the group feels are worth pursuing further. There's a chance that nothing you share will be met with enthusiasm, or that they will say they love everything. Neither of those outcomes is particularly helpful, as they won't help you move forward with your ideas.

The best outcome is often a mixed response, where some of your suggestions are broadly disliked or dismissed, while one or two others are met with genuine interest and enthusiasm. You don't need your colleagues to love everything you suggest, but you are hoping there will be something in there that will get them a little excited.

If your ideas are met with resistance or negativity, don't take that as a failure. Maybe you could schedule another TELL session with some different colleagues, or perhaps you should revisit your ideas and explore how you can make them more palatable for others. After the TELL session, chat with colleagues individually to try to unravel any objections or concerns. When you get to the bottom of their issues, you'll have a clearer sense of what you may need to do differently. Then you can head back to your desk, gather your thoughts, and rework your approach before hosting another TELL session. Most importantly, don't get disheartened or give up at the first try. Learn from the experience and figure out how to keep moving your ideas forward. As a minimum, you should plan to run another TELL session, either to refine your ideas further or to start afresh. If this is your first spin around the ReadyAlready Growth Cycle, you're still learning and can probably improve next time. Use this moment to think about your journey and consider what you will now do differently to gain more support and make faster progress towards your Personal Mission.

Whatever the outcome, you've come this far, so dig in and keep going. Don't throw in the towel just yet! Many of my ideas were met with passive apathy at best on their first airing. That doesn't mean all my ideas were terrible, just that they didn't quite land with the positive impact I was hoping for. With time to reflect, I often figured out the reason why. Maybe the group dynamic was wrong, my presentation fell flat, or my ideas were too ambitious or even ahead of their time. I hope you won't find yourself in that position, but if you do, take some time to think before deciding how to pick yourself up, make a few changes, and then go again. You owe it to your Personal Mission to doggedly pursue what you believe in. A muted response is never a failure; it's just another learning point on your journey. And if you do get a resoundingly positive, celebratory, joyful response, that's not a total success either! There's still work to do to transform ideas into action.

Step 8: Transitioning to action after a successful TELL session.

Hopefully, your TELL session will have gone well and your invited guests will have enjoyed hearing about your *thing* and your ideas to bring improvements to the organisation. With your colleagues onboard, you can transition fully from thinking about your *thing* to getting your TELL group collectively invested in helping you make good changes happen. It will help if you can secure their ongoing support for your proposals and gather suggestions about how to get the resources, budget, or time you may need to test out your ideas. It's also unlikely that you'll be able (or even willing!) to do everything yourself from here, so you may need to get buy-in from colleagues to help along the way, as well as suggestions of who else in the organisation might be supportive. Together, you can now start transforming the positive opportunities for change that you've identified into reality. You may need to get permission or approval from a HIPPO or the big-big boss, or extra budget and resources to put the game into play. Do whatever you have to do, and just keep going. You've worked hard to get to this point, and it's certainly not the end. This is really just the beginning of the most exciting stage of all: seeing your Personal Mission being delivered as your ideas for positive change become a reality!

Reader Recap: TELL.

- **On why you should give yourself a pat on the back.**
  Don't expect gratitude or congratulations from others.
  You're doing this for yourself. So, take a moment to
  give yourself some credit. Recognise how much you've
  done, what you've learned, how far you've travelled.
  Reflect on your accomplishments and remind yourself
  why you're doing this (your Personal Mission). Pause,
  reflect, and celebrate your achievements. Even if
  nothing else comes from this, you have grown as a
  person and built your future-readiness. Keep going,
  you're doing important work!

- **On getting the right vibe in your TELL session.**
  I shared with you earlier that I enjoy building
  my performance muscles by taking part in
  improvisational theatre shows.. 'Yes, and...' is the
  foundation of constructive conversations because it
  shifts the dialogue to positively building on what the
  last person said. It makes contributions additive, not
  destructive. The flip side of 'Yes, and...' is 'Yes, but...'
  or, even worse, 'No, because...' You don't want that
  kind of negativity in your TELL session! Remember
  what Pippa Evans wrote: 'Yes, and...' opens up our
  minds to many amazing possibilities and can be
  thrilling!

- **On making TELL a big part of your work culture.**
  The process of talking about new things and listening

to others' hopes and dreams for the future can be immensely valuable for an organisation's work culture and long-term growth prospects. Some of the companies that I've worked with have made TELL sessions a regular feature, with volunteers stepping forward to talk about their *thing*, and supportive colleagues coming along just for the thrill of learning something new and contributing their ideas. This culture shift works best when this happens almost organically, when enough people are enthusiastic about creating a brighter future, and someone steps forward to coordinate the TELL sessions. Perhaps you could be that person who makes becoming future-ready easier and more fun for your colleagues.

TELL is about communicating with the right people in the right way at the right time, so they will listen to your perspective and collaborate with you to help make your ideas even better. Use the space on this page to jot down your initial thoughts for how you might run your first TELL session. Where might it take place, when, and who will you invite? How will you run the session and how will you inspire those 'Yes and...' responses from your audience? Remember: 'The medium is the message'. The thought and care you put into creating your TELL session will have a significant impact on the eventual outcome.

Conclusion

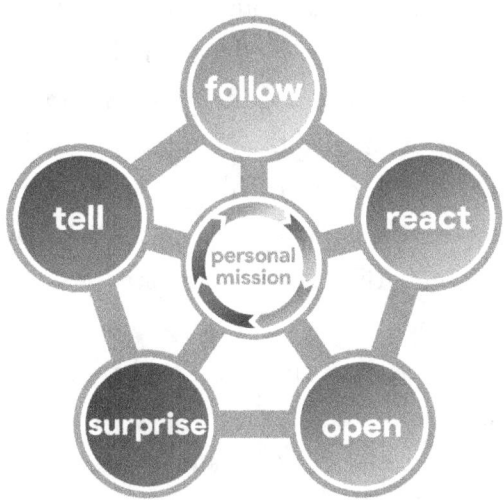

The ReadyAlready Growth Cycle is a simple but powerful process that you can spin again and again to help you become future-ready for life. The more often you do it, the faster you can spin. After your first full cycle (and hopefully some positive outcomes), reflect on what you've learned, then go back to the FOLLOW step, add more things to your list, and select one new *thing* to explore. And away you go again.

With each spin of the cycle, you'll be exploring a new *thing* that you feel may be important in your near future and will support your Personal Mission. You'll be selecting that *thing* from a long list of contenders that you identify during FOLLOW, learning all about it and deciding if it's relevant to your future or not in REACT. And then you'll be unleashing your human superpowers to examine and finesse your *thing* in ways that no computer or AI model can ever do. You'll fire up your curiosity in OPEN, asking naïve 'Why?' questions to challenge the status quo and spot many areas where your *thing* might bring improvements at work. With space opened up in your mind to explore new possibilities, you'll then develop fresh ideas for potential quick wins—and maybe even big wins—in SURPRISE by unleashing your brilliant human creativity and imagining 'What if...?'. And, finally, you'll collaborate with colleagues to share your journey during TELL and ask for their help to say 'Yes, and...' to make your ideas even better and give you the confidence to secure wider support to transform your thoughts into real, positive changes. After you've done it once, you can go again, with a brand new *thing* to focus on. Again and again, ensuring you are always thinking ahead and exploring fresh possibilities for the future. Not just thinking about the future, but creating it with every spin of the ReadyAlready Growth Cycle.

Your Personal Mission doesn't need to change each time you work through the cycle, but it's worth checking in every few months to confirm it's still motivating and relevant to your work. If at some point, your life moves on and you're no longer fully invested in your Personal Mission, find a new one that relights the fire inside you. As I look back on my career, I can remember several pivotal Personal Missions that helped me succeed. And you will too.

What's next? To help you stay focused and to create a special place where you can think about the future, I highly recommend getting yourself a small, pocket-sized notebook and a pen. Carry these with you at all times while you're working through this process. Here's a new rule for a future-ready life: Don't leave home without your keys, phone, and your ReadyAlready notebook and pen! This ever-present notepad can be your special place to capture thoughts and ideas whenever you have time to ponder your future. I've seen how hard it can be to think about the future on your phone or laptop, because those devices regularly drag your thinking back to the present with every new notification or reminder that pops up. A notepad and pen will never interrupt your train of thought and can become your permanent friends on your journey to the future. Every time you're in a coffee shop or on a train, staring out of the window or unthinkingly scrolling through your phone, that little notepad will remind you to think about your future. And each time you open it, you'll see what you last wrote and can instantly pick up where you left off. A paper notebook and pen are always ready to go; make them your friends for the future! And, if nothing else, carrying that little notebook with you will be a constant reminder that there's more to life than today; there's a brilliant future you also need to create!

To see the best results possible from this book and

the ReadyAlready Growth Cycle, you need to start right away. Why not begin by scheduling a TELL session with a few colleagues in two months' time? Having a hard deadline to work towards may help focus your mind and keep you on track. You can always reschedule if your progress slows or races ahead. But, for now, just start and keep going.

Every time you've read something in this book and thought it sounded a bit weird or unusual, that's fine. I thought that too, but when you work through the different steps of the cycle and you get good at it, it will quickly become second nature, and you'll find yourself thinking in this way whenever you spot an opportunity to improve the future.

And here's something that I wish I'd realised much earlier in my career. You may dream up some opportunities for improvement that you have authority and permission to change straight away. However, please don't be a hero like me and think, 'I'll just fix that'. Instead, take the time to share each idea you have with someone else, maybe in a mini, ad hoc TELL session. Just a little sharing to bounce the idea off another helpful human being. You may benefit from their reaction, ideas, and input, and you'll also hear some encouraging validation if they think you're doing the right thing. Don't go solo or hide your ideas and the many improvements, however small, that you bring to the world. Tell others to ensure you get the credit and recognition you deserve.

A lot of people find the idea of a TELL session overwhelming. If that's you, I have a method that will help. Imagine it's nothing more than a 'show and tell' session, like young children sometimes have at school: 'This summer, I went on holiday with my parents, and I bought this spoon. It's from Italy.' Your task is almost as simple. All you have to do is tell people what you've been doing, show them some of your resulting ideas, then invite their questions and observations. If your colleagues are armed with the 'Yes, and...' rule upfront, they will respond with positivity and maybe even come up with some supportive ideas of their own. Remember, you're not trying to reinvent the universe here, you're trying to make some helpful and welcome improvements that others will benefit from. That's all you're doing. Not doing that because of fear, well, that's perhaps the biggest missed opportunity of all.

And finally, you've made a giant leap by taking the time to understand the process and figure out how you will use it to create the future you deserve. Your successes will be hard-earned, but you'll see more and go faster if you can inspire others at work to think the same way and be as proactive as you. If you've finished with this book and feel you no longer need it, pass it on to someone else. Or, tell your colleagues about the ReadyAlready Growth Cycle and help them to get started. When you have a common language for change and growth, your company culture will evolve more quickly. If, just a few months from now, you can have conversations with colleagues about their Personal

Mission, or what *thing* they're working on, or their progress with OPEN or SURPRISE, or how much you are looking forward to the next TELL session, you'll be in a great place where positive change is literally happening all around. Share your experiences, tell others, and together you will create the bright future you truly deserve.

Next Steps

- You can find special bonus resources to help you go faster on your journey to a Future-Ready Mindset at https://ReadyAlready.pro.

- If you'd like extra coaching support or to book Allister Frost to speak at a company meeting or industry event, get in touch at https://allisterspeaks.com/contact.

- To receive Allister's free email newsletter with tips and ideas to help you realise your full future potential, head to https://hello.allisterspeaks.com.

'Remember: the light at the end of the tunnel may be you.'

Amazing, by Aerosmith

About the Author

Allister Frost is a business growth and transformation expert who inspires working professionals to transform ever-accelerating change into collective growth—all to build a brighter tomorrow.

During a two-decade corporate career, he jumped from the relative stability of a leadership role in a global consumer goods company into the wild seas of change at Microsoft. In the emergent technology sector, he developed strategies to help him thrive in uncertainty through continuous reinvention. He became Microsoft's first ever Head of Digital Marketing Strategy, pioneering revolutionary new communication channels and launching new versions of Windows and iconic brand campaigns, including 'I'M A PC'. This is where he first started to develop and codify the powerful new mindset for growth that he now shares in his talks and in this book.

Since 2012, Allister has travelled the world as a motivational speaker and coach to leading organisations including Cisco, the NHS, Hyundai, 3M, Team GB, Airbus, and Bosch. Through hundreds of client projects, he has demonstrated how anyone, regardless of the state of the economy or the nature of their business, can develop a Future-Ready Mindset so they keep up and thrive. He specialises in helping leaders and teams rethink their relationship with change, so they stretch their comfort zones and realise their full potential. He believes everyone can enjoy a lifetime of personal growth and career success when they have the right attitude to change combined with a passion for working in the service of others (their 'Personal Mission').

Allister now shares the secrets of his ReadyAlready Growth Cycle at company conferences and industry events. As a sought-after, award-winning speaker, he helps busy professionals develop a more optimistic relationship with change through his personal story of thriving in uncertainty. He believes there are opportunities for improvement everywhere when you employ more human curiosity, creativity, and better communication. His mission each day is simple: to help people change faster and better with the positive mindset needed to become—and remain—future-ready for life.

In his spare time, Allister is a keen runner, photographer, and student of improvisational comedy. He lives in a leafy village suburb of the eternally congested M25 motorway in Surrey, UK, where his family relies on him to help them enjoy a brilliant future and to put the bins out each Thursday.

Acknowledgements

There are so many people who have inspired and shaped this book—brilliant people who have helped me navigate the seas of change and develop the resiliency to transform life's challenges into opportunities. The biggest thank you goes to Mrs. F for bringing nothing but positive change into my life, and to my children for keeping me grounded and poor. My positive outlook on life comes from too many wonderful former colleagues at Kimberly-Clark and Microsoft to mention, but you know who you are. Thank you. I've learned and continue to learn so much from the hundreds of leaders who have believed in me in recent years, inviting me to inspire their teams with keynote talks and masterclasses. Finally, thank you to my talented fellow professional speakers and to my speaker bureau buddies who work tirelessly to keep me busy, jet-lagged, and happy.

www.ingramcontent.com/pod-product-compliance
Lightning Source LLC
Chambersburg PA
CBHW061152120626
46546CB00005B/2038